D1130897

This library edition published in 2011 by Walter Foster Publishing, Inc.
Walter Foster Library
Distributed by Black Rabbit Books.
P.O. Box 3263 Mankato, Minnesota 56002

Printed in China, Shanghai Offset Printing Products Limited, Shenzhen.

First Library Edition

Library of Congress Cataloging-in-Publication Data

Powell, William F.
  Perspective / by William F. Powell. -- 1st library ed.
      p. cm. -- (Artist's library series)
  ISBN 978-1-936309-28-3 (hardcover)
  1. Perspective. 2. Drawing--Technique. I. Title.
  NC750.P78 2011
  742--dc22

                                                                    2010009449

032010
0P1815

9 8 7 6 5 4 3 2 1

CONTENTS

INTRODUCTION . . . History of Perspective

Perspective in the art of drawing and painting, and in some relief sculpture, is a technique that allows us to represent three-dimensional objects and space on a flat surface or plane. This surface or plane is the board, paper, canvas, or surface onto which we draw or paint our impression and view of an object or scene.

In art, there are a number of ways to use perspective thinking and logic in order to obtain the illusion of depth — some with the use of color and graduated values of black and white, and some with accurate drawing of the subject by applying the rules of the geometric system of perspective.

LINEAR PERSPECTIVE as we know it today is thought to have evolved from the early architectural drawings of two architects, Brunelleschi and Alberti, in Florence, Italy in early 1400 A.D. Filippo Brunelleschi drew two panels that were pictorial views of Florence in perspective. These panels made an important impact on art theory in the areas of architecture and fine art. Unfortunately, the two original panels are lost. Leone Battista Alberti was a painter, musician and architect in Florence, Italy. He designed some of the most classical buildings of the 15th century. He wrote the very first book on painting that covered both theory and technique, and it had a great influence on the Renaissance artists. His writing covered subjects such as imitation of nature, beauty, perspective and ancient art. An interesting side note is that in 1464, Alberti wrote another work on the subject of sculpture. This writing was another first work in the field and covered human proportions.

In his book *De pittura*, Alberti combined the rules and techniques of perspective with the theory that painting is an imitation of reality. He saw the picture plane as a window through which the artist sees the visible three-dimensional world. Objects appeared smaller as they receded into the distance, and objects of uniform distance from one another, such as fence posts, appeared to become closer together the farther they receded into the distance. Projected imaginary lines that were parallel to the surface plane converged to one point at the horizon. All of the objects in the picture related to the same horizon when viewed from the same viewing or station point. In this method, all objects could be measured in proper geometric proportion to one another.

The Italian artists of that day tended to work within this geometric system, while the Flemish artists relied upon their observations and practical experience to accomplish the illusion of depth and space. This is referred to as the empirical method of achieving depth.

Leonardo da Vinci is credited with the general development of the AERIAL or ATMOSPHERIC PERSPEC-TIVE. This method is based upon observations that contrasts of color and values of dark and light are much greater in objects that are close than in ones that are distant. Atmosphere and light affect the colors of objects in nature. A bluish white effect, created by atmosphere, is noticeable on all colors as they become more distant. Also, lines, edges and contours are more clearly defined in objects that are closer than those more distant. Aerial perspective also observes that distance affects the color of objects and that the same color appears cooler and lighter when placed more distant, and warmer and more intense when closer.

The use of linear perspective has had a great influence upon the development of art in the western cultures, but, in the art of today, it is being cast aside by many who feel that art is more an extended expression of themselves than a mirroring of nature and reality. In some cases, I view this as a lazy excuse to avoid the labor of learning to draw.

The knowledge of perspective is invaluable to the serious artist no matter what technique or school of art he or she may prefer. If we know and understand the basic theories of perspective, then we can produce our work in any degree of realism or thoughtful distortion.

In this book it is my intention to present the rules of perspective so that you can use them as a guide in the preparation of your work. This does not mean that you must draw and measure everything to the nth degree, but instead use the rules as a tool to correct a problem if it exists. By knowing perspective, problems of proportions and the relationships of objects one to another that may develop in our drawings are more easily spotted. How often have we said to ourselves, "Something looks wrong in my painting, but I just can't seem to put my finger on it." With an understanding of perspective, you will immediately know how to correct any distortion that may appear.

In this study of perspective, I would like to suggest that you do not skip around in the book, but follow it thoroughly, step-by-step, as it has been carefully organized into a progressive study.

I truly hope you will enjoy it.

PERSPECTIVE . . . How Does It Work?

Perspective is a method of drawing and painting the illusion of depth onto a flat surface. In order to do this, we must make a number of observations.

The forms or objects that we are drawing onto that flat surface actually, in real life, have depth and dimension. As we view them and place their shapes and forms onto our drawing surface, we must always try to represent that depth so as to make the objects appear real and true. These forms must appear to extend deeply into the illusional space of our picture in order to create the only true magic in drawing and painting — the appearance of form, depth and the natural play of light — all on a flat surface.

In the examples, notice that one of the arrows and one of the roads appear to have depth while the others appear flat.

 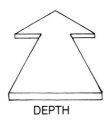  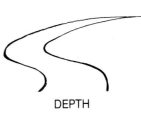

NO DEPTH   DEPTH   NO DEPTH   DEPTH

The foundation of all good paintings and drawings, no matter how beautifully shaded and colored, is the correctness of perspective in the drawing of the form and the depth of the objects portrayed.

SKETCH SHOWING
VISIBLE SURFACES

In order to make the task of obtaining depth and form easier, we should think about the whole object we are drawing. Do not just look at the front visible surface, but imagine the complete object as the planes of the sides recede. Objects that have depth and breadth have backs and other sides. In order to feel this, we must study the object and draw the feeling of the complete form. If we want to draw a box, we should sketch it as if it were transparent. By drawing this way, we not only understand the box better, but are more likely to draw it correctly in size and shape. We certainly will be able to portray the illusion of depth far easier this way than if we just concentrated on the *visible surface*.

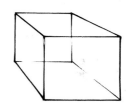

SAME OBJECT WITH ALL
PLANES SKETCHED

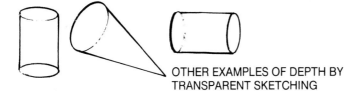

OTHER EXAMPLES OF DEPTH BY
TRANSPARENT SKETCHING

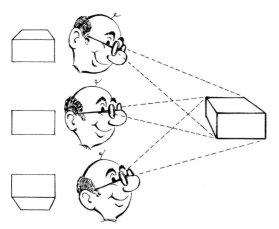

Objects appear very different when viewed from various positions. Because of this, we must establish our viewing point (the position from which we view the subject) and stick with it for the complete picture. When we observe our subject, we see depth and three dimensions. When we draw this subject onto our flat surface as it appears to the eye, we are then DRAWING IN PERSPECTIVE.

3

The first thing to remember is to freehand your drawings as much as possible, but use perspective to check for accuracy or to establish a very involved subject. If we rely on perspective too much and omit the freedom of sketching by eye, our work will take on a stiff, mechanical appearance.

Some tools that are helpful are a T-square, a triangle, and a compass. There are also sets of ellipse guides at various degrees of angle, circle guides, ships curves and so forth. These are very expensive, and unless you are planning to go into mechanical and technical illustration, I would suggest sticking with the simple tools. A string and thumbtacks are handy for placing a vanishing point somewhere far out of our picture plane and reach.

With a drawing board, a T-square, a triangle, thumbtacks and string as tools, and freehand sketching by eye, we can draw anything we encounter.

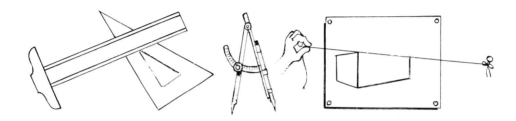

We must draw the objects in proper proportions and distances into the picture, as well as in proper relationship to other objects.

The rules of perspective enable us to draw and paint scenes or objects so as to show them as they really appear to the eye. This is all with reference to shape and form, positioning, distance, depth and relationship with all other objects. Also, perspective allows us to study and analyze the proportions of areas *within* a larger mass for size and correctness of shape.

All of the rules of perspective are easy to understand. There are several basic rules we will study. As we study these rules, apply them to the objects in your home and the things around you every day. You will be amazed at what you will start to observe. It is not only my desire to share the basic rules of perspective with you, but also to assist you in *really seeing* what you are looking at. A new world will open to you and your drawings and paintings will take on a tremendous new look! Even if you paint in the abstract, understanding the rules of perspective will be a tremendous help in the relationships of forms.

As described in the introduction, there are several approaches to the study of perspective. In this book, we will study the most geometric set of rules — linear perspective. We will not forget the other approaches, however, since they are all relative.

The main observation to consider is that *all objects appear to be smaller the farther away they are from your point of viewing.* Also, any portions of the object that are *farther away appear smaller than the parts that are nearest to our eye.* All of the objects appear to be receding to a common line. That line is the horizon. If we have a number of objects that are the same space apart, such as fence posts, the space between them appears to lessen as the objects become smaller with distance. The farther away an object appears, the closer to the horizon it will be. In the sky, the same rule applies — the closer to the horizon an object is, the more distant it appears.

These are some of the basic rules of observation that we will be using in this study of perspective. Remember, the rules of perspective are easy and I know that you will find them as fascinating and helpful in your work as I do in mine.

PERSPECTIVE TERMS . . .

Now that we know *what* perspective is, we need to understand the rules and how to apply them. In order to make the study easier, I would like to explain some of the terms that will be used. Once you become acquainted with these terms, the subject of perspective will seem easier. Remember, perspective really is easy. Just follow the rules, step-by-step.

SUBJECT: We all know that the term "subject" refers to the object or scene that we are dealing with in the composition of our drawing or painting. It can be one item or many things, such as a complex scene from nature. Whichever it is, we must try and present that subject so as to create a pleasant picture. Using perspective as an aid in deciding how to best portray the subject is very helpful. Make sure that you have chosen a subject that you *really* have a desire to draw or you might lose interest in it along the way and never complete the work because the initial excitement with the subject waned. All of us have experienced the feeling of excitement at the beginning of a work only to have it wane as we progress into the labor of actually doing it. It is up to us to reach out and yank back that enthusiasm we felt in the beginning so as to make the work what we had hoped it would be. If we don't, it will turn out looking labored. So, select your subject carefully and realize how much work there will be in bringing it to a completed piece. By following through in this manner, we experience a rewarding sense of accomplishment.

PICTURE PLANE: The "picture plane" is simply the surface area of the picture. The edges of the picture are the limits, or edges, of the picture plane. In the introduction I discussed how Alberti saw the "picture plane" as a window through which the artist sees the visible three-dimensional world. That window is the surface of our drawing.

The surface of the paper is a two-dimensional plane. When a drawing of a three-dimensional object is made on this two-dimensional surface, it becomes the picture plane. The illusion of depth and form have been drawn on a flat surface. We must always view the subject as if through a transparent vertical plane and transfer what is seen to the flatness of the picture plane surface without ever forgetting *depth* and *form*. In the illustration, the canvas appears to be a window through which the artist is viewing the subject. This is a simple, but good, example of the artist using the picture plane to transfer the illusion of depth to the flat surface of the drawing.

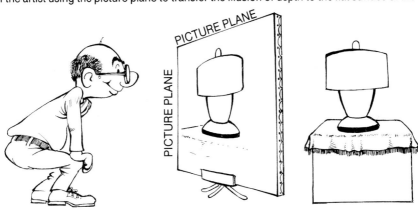

PICTURE PLANE

PICTURE PLANE

An easy way to experience the value of the picture plane is to use a real window at home. Take a grease pencil and draw a border approximately 9" x 12" on the window. The area within the outline is the picture plane. The outline is the border. Now, stand in one spot and, without moving your position, draw the outlines of what you see in the picture plane area on the window. You have just drawn three-dimensional depth and form on a flat surface. You have created exactly what you would on your paper or canvas by using the imaginary picture plane. It's fun! Try a few different windows and views, then you will really begin to understand the term, "picture plane."

VIEWING POINT AND ANGLE AND ELEVATION OF VIEW: Every object appears different when viewed from various angles. In order to create a realistic illusion of the subject, we must view it and all other relating objects from the same viewing point. The viewing point can be seen as a straight line from our eye to the horizon line. If we move to the right or left, we are changing the viewing point and there will be major changes in the drawing. The place where we stand to look at the subject is known as the *viewing point* and must remain constant. When you are drawing on the window pane, you probably noticed that if you moved very much, the drawing became distorted and difficult to accomplish. Try changing your position in relation to the outline of the window and notice the vast difference in the subject matter and its placement in the picture plane. When the angle of the viewing point is changed, either to the right or to the left, the entire picture is changed.

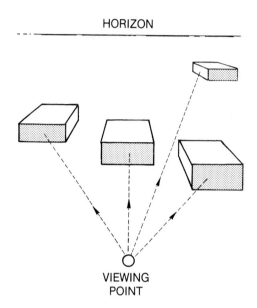

HORIZON

VIEWING
POINT

IF THE BOX IS PLACED IN DIFFERENT POSITIONS, OUR VIEW CHANGES, AND SO DOES THE SHAPE. THE SHAPE CHANGES ALSO IF WE MOVE OUR VIEWING POINT.

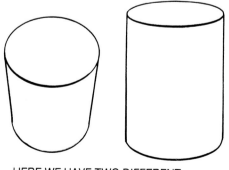

HERE WE HAVE TWO DIFFERENT VIEWS OF THE SAME CYLINDER. WE SEE MORE OF THE TOP OF THE LEFT ONE BECAUSE WE HAVE A HIGHER ELEVATION OF VIEW.

The same is true if the elevation from which the subject is viewed is changed. If the elevation is raised, the view of the subject is downward. If the elevation is lowered, the view is upward. The slightest degree of change in the elevation of view will create drastic differences in how we perceive all of the objects in the picture. If a cylinder is viewed from the top, the view is a foreshortened one and will result in a completely different drawing than one of the same cylinder viewed from the side. Here are two examples of the results of changing elevations of view of the same cylinder. Once selected, the elevation of view must be kept constant. Always try to select the elevation of view that will best portray the subject.

HORIZON LINE: The horizon is represented by the point at which the sea and sky, or flat land and sky, meet. This is the natural and true horizon. The true horizon line is always at the *level* of your eyes and will change as you change the elevation of view. The higher the elevation of view, the higher the horizon line will be on the picture plane, showing more ground and less sky. The lower the elevation of view, the lower the horizon line will be on the picture plane; thus, more sky than ground will be seen. So, the position of the horizon line in our picture depends on the elevation from which we view the subject. Notice the change in position of the apple on the canvas with the different elevations of view.

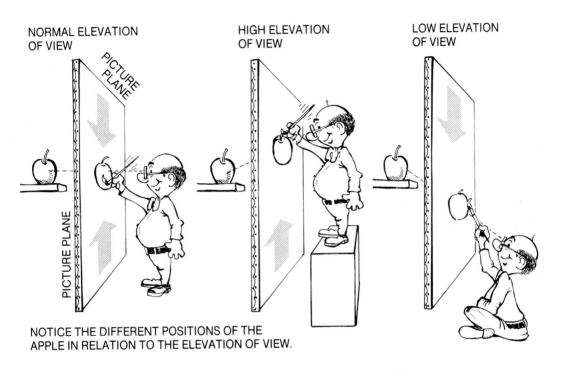

NORMAL ELEVATION OF VIEW

HIGH ELEVATION OF VIEW

LOW ELEVATION OF VIEW

NOTICE THE DIFFERENT POSITIONS OF THE APPLE IN RELATION TO THE ELEVATION OF VIEW.

There are times when the true horizon line cannot be seen. A good example of this would be when we are in a room looking at a table with a box on it. The walls of the room hide the true horizon. Even though we can't see it, it is there and must always be kept in mind in order to draw the subject correctly. Any object that is level and parallel to the ground plane will be affected by the horizon line.

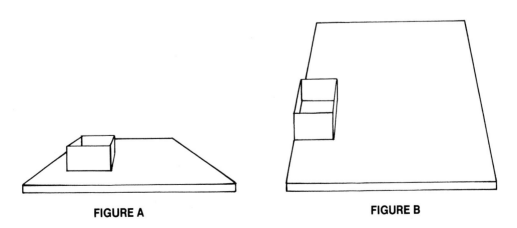

FIGURE A

FIGURE B

VANISHING POINT: Lines that are parallel to one another and level with the ground plane, such as furrows in a plowed field, appear to meet at the same point on the horizon line. This point is known as the vanishing point. The vanishing point is one of the most important points to establish accurately in order to draw the object accurately. If a vanishing point is misplaced, the object will be distorted in the drawing.

Look at a long table from one end and notice that the far end appears to be smaller than the near end. We know that the ends of the table are the same width, but due to perspective, we notice the viewing difference. This is the *illusion of depth* as shown by perspective (Figure A).

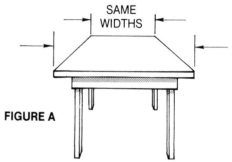

FIGURE A

If we draw imaginary lines along the sides of the table and extend them out towards the horizon, they will meet on the horizon line. If we then put a dot at the point where they meet, we have established a vanishing point (Figure B).

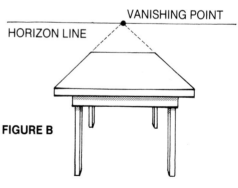

FIGURE B

Lines that are parallel to the table side lines will also meet at the same vanishing point on the horizon line. All objects in the picture will also seem to grow smaller as they move into the picture, toward the horizon line (Figure C). So, the horizon line plays a number of important roles in the rules of perspective. Now that we have a basic understanding of some of the terms used in perspective, let's consider the types of perspective, and the ones that are most important to us.

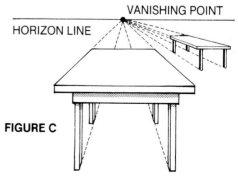

FIGURE C

ONE-POINT PERSPECTIVE . . .

In many of the objects we might select to draw and paint, we find there are three types of perspective that we use most. They are: one-point, two-point and three-point perspective. We will study all three of these and they will usually suffice for the average subject matter. There are, however, objects that are not of the simple form and are made up of a complex number of sides and faces. These are known as complex forms and we will discuss them a little later in the study. To begin with, we will concentrate on one-, two- and three-point perspectives.

As discussed in the previous section, we know that lines which are parallel to one another, and recede into the depth of the picture toward the horizon, will all meet at one point on the horizon line. This point is the vanishing point and is *used for all objects in one-point perspective*. Also, we have one-point perspective when both the height and width of an object are parallel to the picture plane (Figure A). When an object is placed in this position it is viewed straight on. The edges of the front, top, bottom and sides of the object are parallel to the edges of the picture plane. They have no depth; therefore, they have no lines that extend to a vanishing point (Figure A).

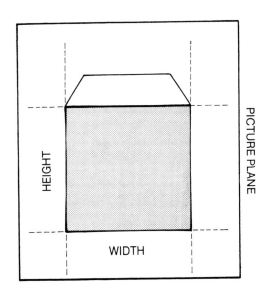

FIGURE A

The surfaces, such as the sides, top, and bottom, that extend into the picture creating the illusion of depth have extended imaginary lines that will join at the vanishing point on the horizon line. When looking at a cube straight on, we see that the edges of the top extend into the picture and meet at the vanishing point, giving the illusion of depth (Figure B). Study and practice the examples. Notice that there are a number of ways to view a simple cube in one-point perspective.

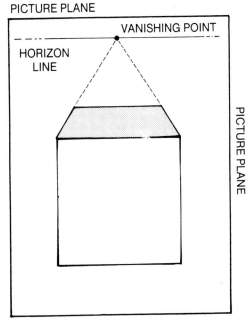

FIGURE B

Drawing a Cube in One-Point Perspective

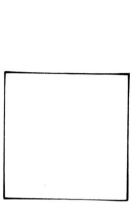

Step 1. Lightly sketch the general shape of the face of the cube.

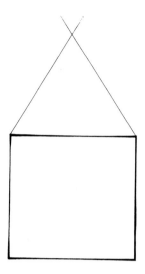

Step 2. Lightly draw the two angle lines along the top until they cross.

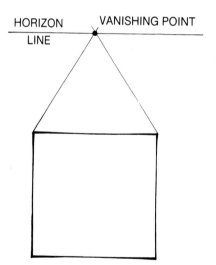

Step 3. At the point where they cross, draw a horizontal line parallel to the top and bottom lines of the cube. This is the horizon line.

Now, place a vanishing point where the lines cross. (This is the way to find the horizon line and vanishing point using the angles from an object — a cube, a table, et cetera.)

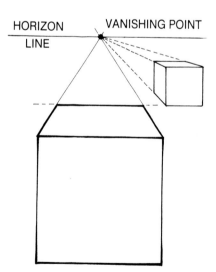

Step 4. Draw a parallel line between the horizon line and the top of the cube. This establishes the top surface of the cube. Darken the lines. Here is a cube drawn in perfect one-point perspective.

Drawing the Inside

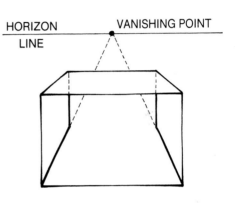

Step 1. Here is a box that will appear to be open with the front off. By extending lines from the left and right corners to the vanishing point, we establish lines for the floor and side walls.

Step 2. Draw vertical lines down from the back left and right corners. The width of the back wall is now established. Darken the lines as shown. This makes the side walls.

Step 3. Draw a horizontal line from the back left corner to the right one. This gives us the width of the back wall in true one-point perspective.

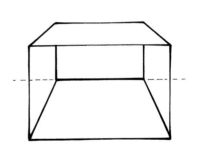

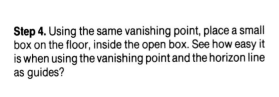

Step 4. Using the same vanishing point, place a small box on the floor, inside the open box. See how easy it is when using the vanishing point and the horizon line as guides?

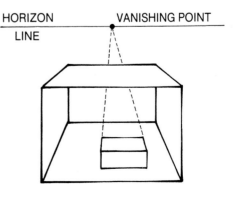

Exercises to Practice

If we view the cube in an elevated position, the vanishing point and horizon line would be in this position, below the cube. By being placed this way, it gives the cube the illusion of flying.

HL = HORIZON LINE
VP = VANISHING POINT

HL

VP

VP

HL

In the exercise above, a number of boxes of various sizes and positions are drawn using the same perspective point. Notice that in all cases, the height and the width of the boxes are always parallel to the picture plane.

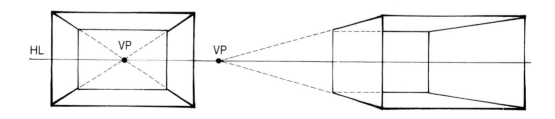

HL   VP   VP

Here is an inside view of a box when we see it straight on and the horizon line crosses through it. The horizon line is there, we just can't see it. There is no need for a vanishing point until we look *into* the box. Notice that by establishing the horizon line and vanishing point, we can now draw the inside of the box, giving us perspective depth. This could be the inside of a room and we would see the ceiling, floor, side walls and end wall. The box on the right has simply been drawn as if placed farther to the right from the viewing and vanishing points.

Step 1. As we know, by establishing a horizon line and a vanishing point we can draw objects in proper size, shape and relationship to one another. Here, a simple rectangular box is shown. It could turn into a house or a refrigerator or any other object that fits that shape.

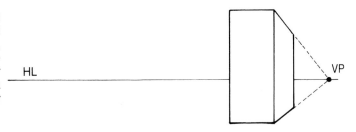

Step 2. Using the same perspective point, we have added another form. Now the boxes have started to take on the appearance of buildings.

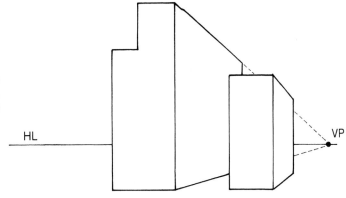

Step 3. By drawing horizontal lines parallel to the horizon, and depth guidelines to the vanishing point, we have drawn streets. By using the vanishing point, we draw windows and start to turn the rectangled boxes into buildings. The way to get the proper distance between windows is discussed in the section titled "Measurements."

Step 1. Draw a straight horizontal line to represent the width of the top front edge nearest you.

Step 2. Lightly draw the angle of the top left side receding into the picture.

Step 3. Lightly draw the angle of the top right side receding into the picture.

Where the lines cross, place a vanishing point and draw the horizon line.

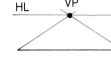

Step 4. Now connect the two sides by drawing a horizontal line for the back edge and you have drawn the top of the table in perspective. Darken your lines.

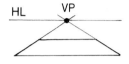

Step 5. Draw two short vertical lines for the sides of the top.

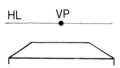

Step 6. Connect them with a horizontal line and there is the end of the table.

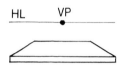

Step 7. Draw the front of the two legs as shown. Make sure they are exactly the same length.

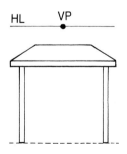

Step 8. Lightly extend two depth guidelines from the inside bottom of each leg to the vanishing point. Then, extend guidelines from the top of the legs to the vanishing point, as shown.

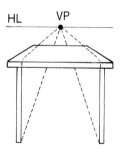

Step 9. Where the top guidelines cross the back edge of the table, draw two vertical lines down to meet the bottom guidelines. This gives us the proper length of the back legs. Now, draw two vertical lines for the depth of the front legs.

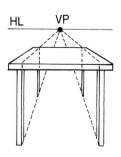

Step 10. Draw two guidelines from the bottom outside corner of each front leg to the V.P. This determines the width of the back legs. Now, place two boxes on the table using the same vanishing point.

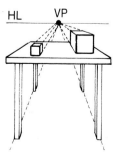

Here, the open cube is shown with items placed in it. This is a good example of one-point perspective showing the horizontal and vertical lines that parallel the picture plane; therefore, having no vanishing point. It is easy to see the lines that *do* recede to the vanishing point giving the illusion of depth as we discussed on page eight under "Vanishing Point."

Notice that you do not see the horizon line due to the walls, but it is established by using your *eye level*. As we already know, the horizon line is always at eye level and the vanishing point is placed on the wall at the very point we see the wall when looking straight ahead. If we turn while looking straight ahead and face another wall, the vanishing point and horizon line would move to eye level and the point we look at on *that* wall. The vanishing point is lightly placed at this spot on the wall and all objects that are viewed straight on and parallel to the horizon line will be drawn using this vanishing point.

Practice drawing this room and then practice on a room in your home. Remember, that in order to use ONE-POINT PERSPECTIVE you must face the wall straight on and not at an angle. Take your time and I am sure that you will find it very easy. The more you practice, the clearer perspective will become. Relax and make a game of it — it is fun to see these things develop.

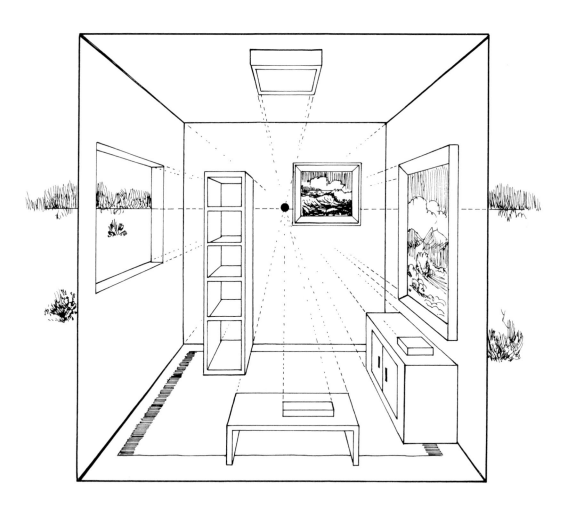

Here is a view of the old Santa Fe railroad station in San Bernardino, California. By standing so as to look down the tracks, we establish a one-point perspective composition. Notice that the railroad ties are parallel to the horizon and the tracks recede into the distance to meet the horizon. The old station on the left is parallel to the tracks and becomes smaller as it recedes into the depth of the picture. Also, note the poles on the right and their diminishing heights as they become distant.

This is one of the beautiful entrances to Balboa Park in San Diego, California. From this viewing point, we have established a one-point perspective composition. The road moves through the arch to the horizon and a vanishing point. Notice the difference in the heights of the lamps as they recede into the picture. Use the lamps to find the horizon line and vanishing point.

TWO-POINT PERSPECTIVE . . .

In one-point perspective, the height *and* the width of the object are parallel to the picture plane. In two-point perspective, *only the height is parallel to the picture plane.* The other dimension, the two sides, recedes into the picture depth; therefore, it must have a set of imaginary extension lines and vanishing points. These vanishing points will also be established on the horizon line. The farther apart the points, the more we see of the sides. The closer together the points, the less we see of the sides. In order to keep our proportions fairly close to reality, we should lightly sketch in the general cubic form of the object and use the sketch to judge how much of each side we really see. Judge one side against the other. In most cases, we see more of one side than the other. Notice that the parallel sides of the cube now appear smaller as they move into the depth of the picture plane. Our viewing point is also established and will remain constant for all objects placed in the picture (Figure A).

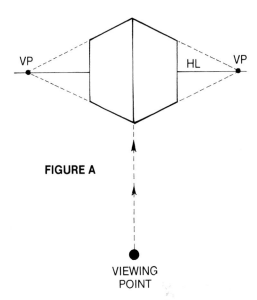

FIGURE A

VIEWING POINT

Instead of viewing the cube from a straight on approach as in one-point perspective, in two-point perspective we are viewing it from an angle. If we could look down and observe ourselves viewing these cubes, this is what we would see (Figure B). In two-point perspective, the corner of the cube is the point closest to us. When we draw the angles of the top and bottom edges of the sides, the extended lines meet on the horizon line, establishing the vanishing points. The vanishing points are usually placed outside of the picture plane or distortion may occur in the drawing (Figure C). If, however, we see a good deal more of one side than the other, one of the vanishing points would be inside of the picture plane and one would be outside.

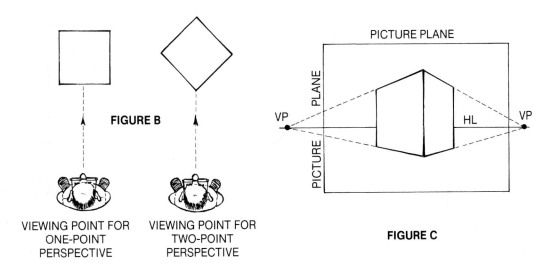

FIGURE B

VIEWING POINT FOR ONE-POINT PERSPECTIVE

VIEWING POINT FOR TWO-POINT PERSPECTIVE

FIGURE C

Drawing a Box in Two-Point Perspective

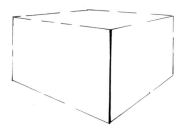

Step 1. Lightly sketch the general shape of the box. Notice that the corner is the closest part . . . darken that line.

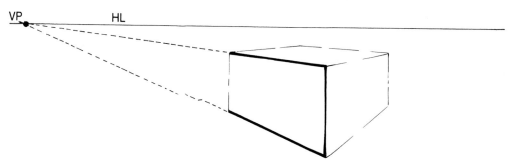

Step 2. Extend the top and bottom lines of the left side. At the point where the lines cross, draw the horizon line and place a vanishing point there.

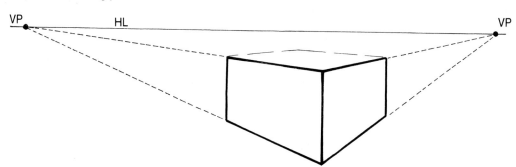

Step 3. Draw in the top and bottom lines of the right side, and place a vanishing point where they meet the horizon line. (They *must* meet.) Now draw the two vertical lines that are the back edges of the sides. This establishes the length of the sides.

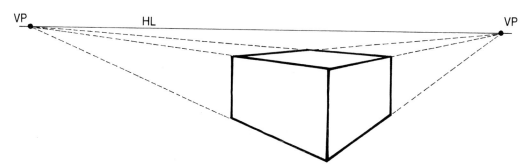

Step 4. Now draw the two top lines using the vanishing points. The top surface is automatically created at the point where they cross at the back of the box.

Drawing the Inside

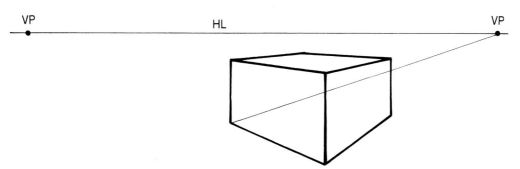

Step 1. Using the box we just drew, draw a light extension line from the bottom left corner to the right vanishing point.

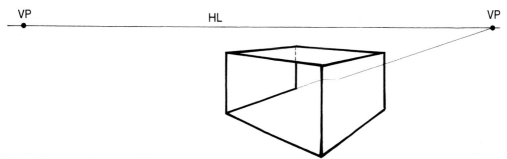

Step 2. Now extend a vertical line down from the back top corner. The point where it intersects the other extension line is the rear corner. Darken the two lines to form the left wall.

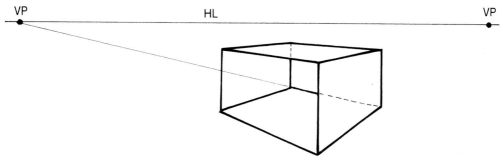

Step 3. By extending a line from the left vanishing point to the bottom right rear corner, we establish the floor and back wall. All of these corners, seen and unseen, must meet.

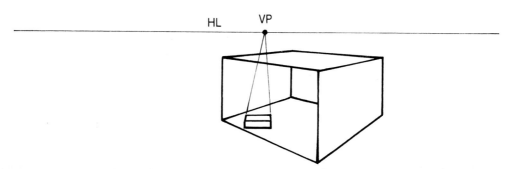

Step 4. Now using one-point perspective, place a box inside this one. This combines the two types of perspective.

Exercises to Practice

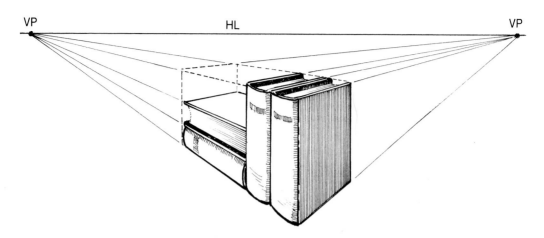

In this exercise, notice how we can turn the simple rectangular forms into objects. Here we have books as they appear in two-point perspective. Almost any form can be blocked in using the cube and rectangle shapes as guides. Try an object in your room, starting with the outside cubic shape for the major form. After it is sketched in, develop the individual shape of the object within the cubic outline. Notice how helpful blocking in can be rather than trying to develop the detail of the object first.

In the example below there are a number of boxes in the same picture, each one on a slightly different elevation. The ones that are placed parallel to one another all use the same set of vanishing points. The one that is at a different angle requires its own vanishing point.

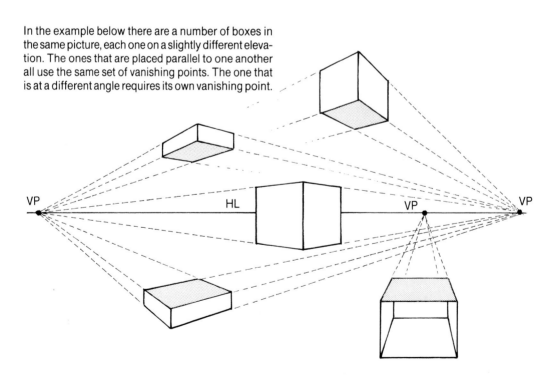

With the addition of the open box on the right, we have a combination of one- and two-point perspective in the same picture. This is very natural and occurs often in nature. Add a few more of your own for practice.

Here are some examples of changing vanishing point placement. As we see more of the right side of the cube, we see less of the left, and the vanishing points move accordingly. Practice drawing other positions using the cube as the subject. Also, place some cubes above and below the horizon line.

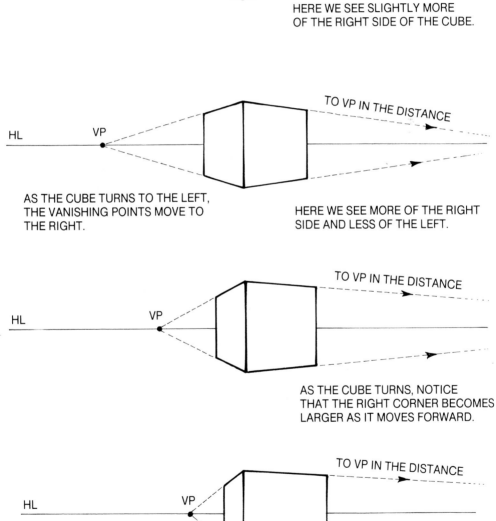

HERE WE SEE SLIGHTLY MORE
OF THE RIGHT SIDE OF THE CUBE.

AS THE CUBE TURNS TO THE LEFT,
THE VANISHING POINTS MOVE TO
THE RIGHT.

HERE WE SEE MORE OF THE RIGHT
SIDE AND LESS OF THE LEFT.

AS THE CUBE TURNS, NOTICE
THAT THE RIGHT CORNER BECOMES
LARGER AS IT MOVES FORWARD.

NOW WE SEE MUCH LESS OF THE
LEFT SIDE. NOTICE THE LEFT
CORNER BECOMING SMALLER.

As we saw in one-point perspective, drawing a city scene or any combination of boxes is easy. Once the first object is placed, all others will relate to it. By establishing a horizon line and vanishing points, we can place a rectangular box onto the ground plane in two-point perspective. Notice that the center front corner is the closest point to us.

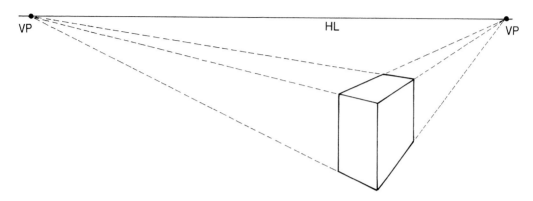

Using the same perspective points, add more boxes of various shapes and sizes. Now they start to look like buildings, as did the boxes in the one-point exercise. Compare the difference in views. Some of the extension lines have been omitted for the sake of clarity.

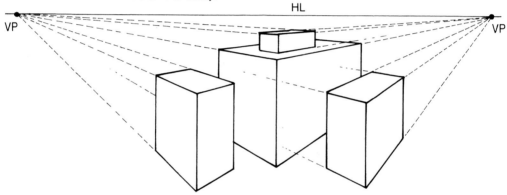

Now, by drawing lines to each vanishing point, we lay in areas of streets and the starting placement of windows and other objects. The distance between the windows is discussed in the section titled "Measurements." As a practice exercise, place some empty boxes of different sizes on the floor and draw them. If they are placed parallel to one another, they will use the same vanishing points.

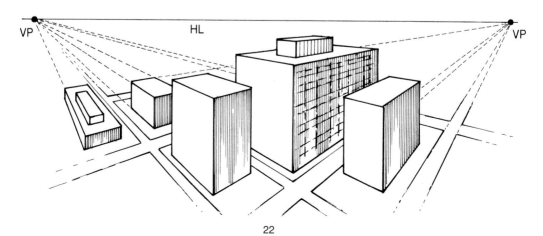

Here is the cube as a room, viewed from the inside. The far corner is vertical and the lines for the right wall extend to the left vanishing point. The lines for the left wall extend to the right vanishing point. The point where each meets on the horizon line is a vanishing point. Any other lines that are parallel to these would use the same vanishing points.

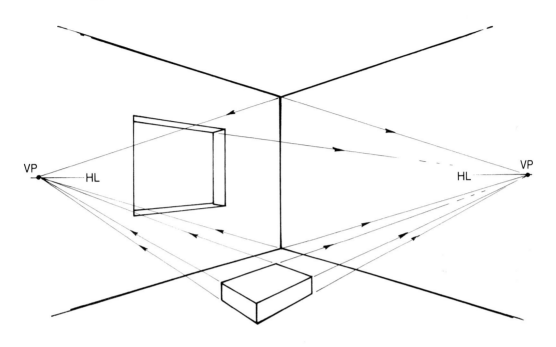

Here is another view of an inside scene using two-point perspective. This one has two rooms with a doorway to look through. Notice that the only lines parallel to the picture plane are the ones indicating height. Only a few extension lines are drawn for the sake of clarity. Also notice that the subject in the painting on the wall has its own horizon line and set of vanishing points. It is, however, still affected by the ones for the room too.

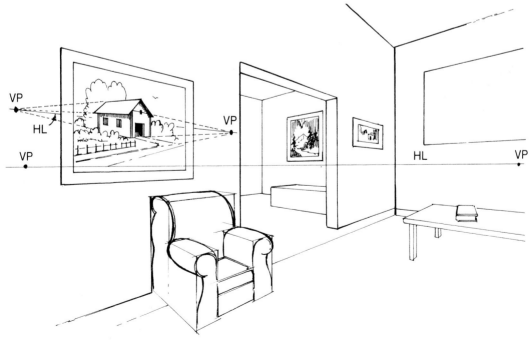

This photo of my wife, Beverly, our dog, Freddie, and me is such a good example of two-point perspective that I had to include it. Follow the lines of the eaves and the boards and the vanishing points are easily established. They then establish the horizon line.

In this close-up of the roof and gables, notice the complexity of all of the different angles. These all still fit into the two-point perspective method of drawing. The method of finding the correct angle for the gables and where they join the roof can be found on page 31 in the section on measurements. Use the same method as above to find the vanishing points and horizon line in this more extreme angle of view.

MEASUREMENTS . . .

Methods of Measuring

Now that we understand the basics of one- and two-point perspective, it is time to discuss how to make proportions correct by measuring. In all drawings, care must be taken to insure that the proportions are correct. In order to do this we must be aware of some methods of measuring not only the object, but areas *within* the object. For instance, the top of the cube must be the right size and shape in comparison to the sides and front. All objects are relative to one another and can be measured against each other. For example, if there is a cup and a large book on a table in a roomful of objects, we would start with the cup. By drawing the cup correctly, we could then compare the book to it. How many cups wide and tall is the book? Then, how many

books tall and wide is the table? Then how many tables wide and tall is the room, and so on. With this method, we can draw everything seen by starting with the smallest object and progressing to the largest.

There are a number of ways to make measurements, but the first order of business for the geometric method is to establish the vanishing point or points and the correct angle and elevation of view. These then establish the horizon line. If this is not done, the exercise will just be a guessing game and there will be no way to prove the correctness of the subject.

Here is a simple method of making measurements: The *visual method* of measuring is to use your pencil and thumb. Always hold the pencil straight out at

arm's length as this is always constant. Use your thumb and measure a small object. Then, using that known measurement, draw several larger objects by counting how many of the small objects fit into the larger. This is also a good method for measuring the distance between objects.

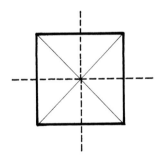

Proportions and Divisions

To find the center of a square, draw diagonal lines from corner to corner. The point where they cross is the center.

In perspective, the square is at an angle, but the same method of finding the center is used.

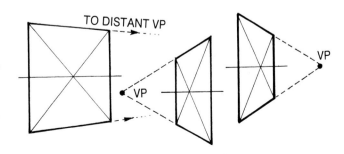

TO DISTANT VP

VP

VP

To divide a portion of the square, the same method is employed, as shown.

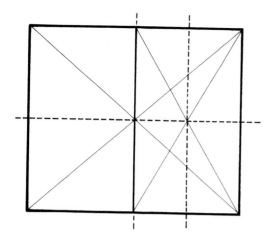
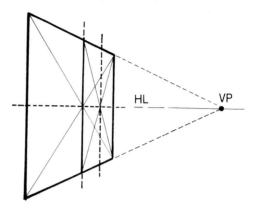

By using this method the area can be divided into as many parts as you wish — squares, rectangles, etc.

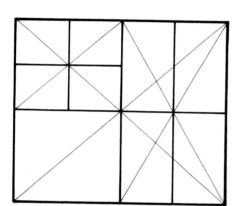
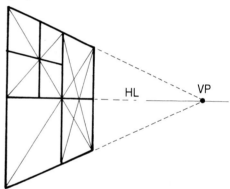

No matter what the angle of perspective is, the same method works.

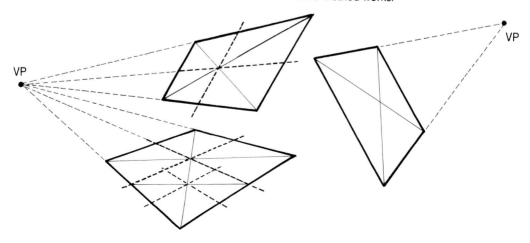

Dividing Areas

If we need to divide the side of an area, like the side of a building for the placement of windows with the proper size and the shortened distance between them as they recede into the depth of the picture, the following method is an easy one to use. In order to divide an area such as this, we must rely upon a line in the drawing that is parallel to the picture plane, either the horizontal base, the top of the object, or the vertical side lines.

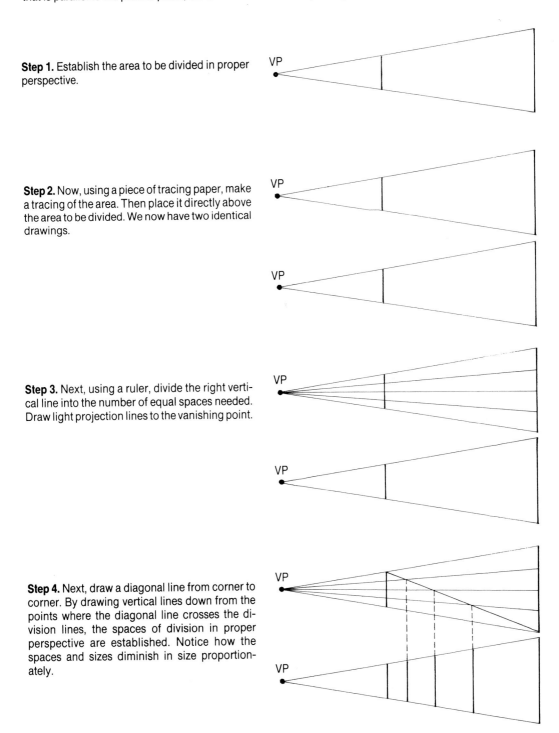

Step 1. Establish the area to be divided in proper perspective.

Step 2. Now, using a piece of tracing paper, make a tracing of the area. Then place it directly above the area to be divided. We now have two identical drawings.

Step 3. Next, using a ruler, divide the right vertical line into the number of equal spaces needed. Draw light projection lines to the vanishing point.

Step 4. Next, draw a diagonal line from corner to corner. By drawing vertical lines down from the points where the diagonal line crosses the division lines, the spaces of division in proper perspective are established. Notice how the spaces and sizes diminish in size proportionately.

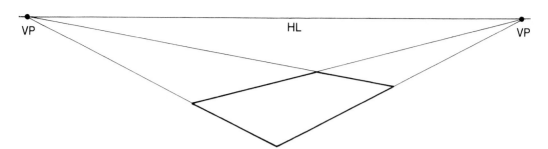

In order to divide a flat surface, such as a tile floor, into proper segments, use the following example.

Draw the area to be divided using two-point perspective.

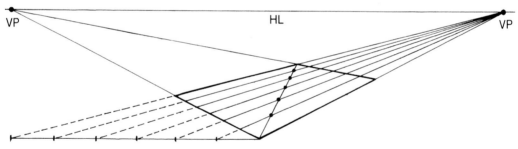

Next, establish the width of the divisions by placing a horizontal line at the bottom of the area and dividing it into equal portions. Now, draw the receding depth lines from the points on the line to the vanishing point on the right.

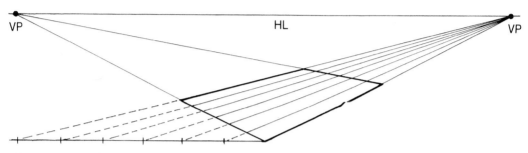

Next, draw a diagonal line from corner to corner and notice that it crosses the depth lines. This establishes the correct depth of each tile.

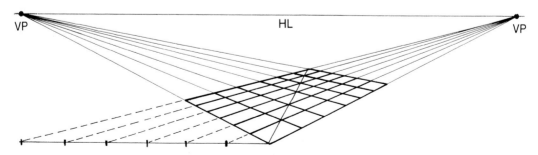

Now, extend lines from these points of contact to the vanishing point on the left and we have a tile floor complete and in correct perspective.

Fence posts, railroad ties, cracks in sidewalks, telephone poles or any other objects that are equally spaced apart are drawn correctly by using the following example of proportional division.

First, establish the horizon line and the vanishing point toward which the posts will be receding. Then, draw the first post in the position desired.

Draw a line from the top and bottom of the first post to the vanishing point. This gives the height guidelines for all posts. Now draw the second post by using visual measurement to establish how far apart they are.

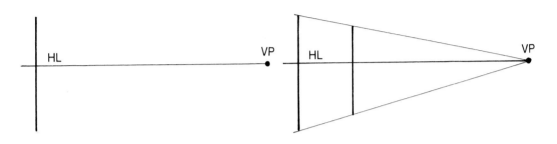

Next, find the middle of the first post and draw a line from that point to the vanishing point.

Next, draw a line from the top of the first post through the center point of the second post and where this line crosses the bottom line, is the location of the next post.

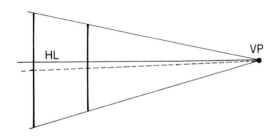
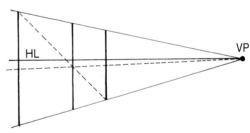

Repeat this procedure as often as necessary to establish the rest of the posts.

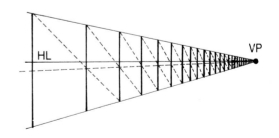

See how easy it is! Try some exercises of your own and do not be afraid to waste paper practicing. The more you practice, the more experienced your eye will become and you will find that you are seeing and drawing more accurately than ever before. Most of the time you will be measuring and drawing using eye judgements and most of the time you will be right. If something does not look quite right, the knowledge of perspective and the methods of proportional measurements are extremely helpful in finding and correcting the error.

Finding the Peak and Pitch of a Roof

First, draw the general shape of the house in the transparent manner, drawing the front and the back walls. Notice the difference in them due to the change in depth.

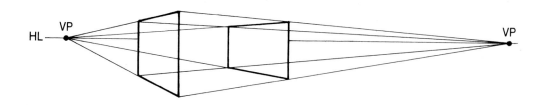

To find the point of the roof, draw a line from each corner to the other. This gives us the exact center of the front and back of the house. Next, draw a vertical guideline for the true center line extending above the walls.

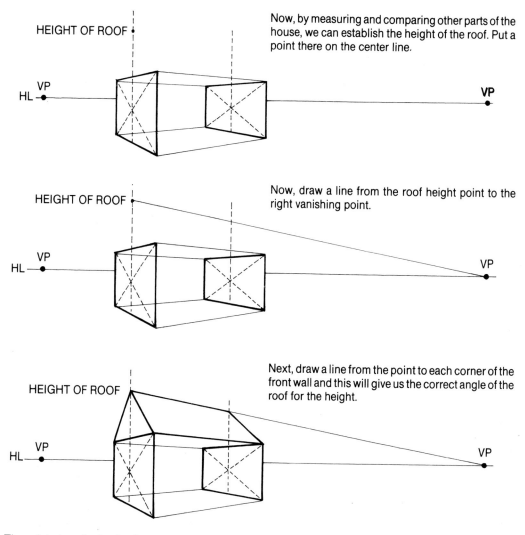

HEIGHT OF ROOF

Now, by measuring and comparing other parts of the house, we can establish the height of the roof. Put a point there on the center line.

HEIGHT OF ROOF

Now, draw a line from the roof height point to the right vanishing point.

HEIGHT OF ROOF

Next, draw a line from the point to each corner of the front wall and this will give us the correct angle of the roof for the height.

The point where the line for the top of the roof crosses the back vertical center line marks the point and pitch of the roof at the back of the house.

This is a simple example of the use of two-point perspective in placement and layout of objects. The road, barn, trees, fence and furrows are all developed from two vanishing points.

Notice the placement and size changes of the trees in relation to one another. By using the base and top points of the front tree and drawing lines from them to the vanishing point, we have a guide for as many trees as we wish. Remember that all trees are not the same height, but this method gives us a rule of perspective that will allow us to measure and use good compositional judgement when placing all of the other trees in our picture.

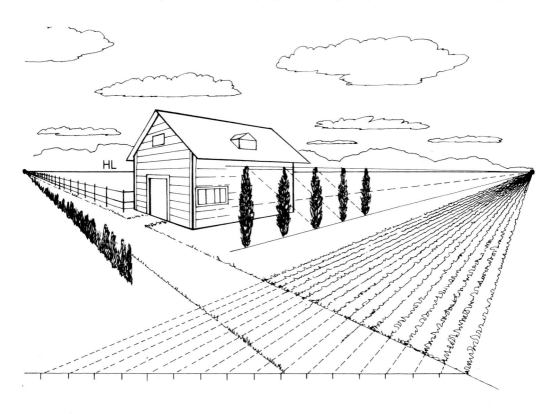

To find the proper angle of the back of the gabled roof, simply extend the front center line back at the same angle as the pitch of the roof. The point where the top roof line and the center line meet is the point of contact with the barn roof. Now, draw a line as shown and there is the correct angle.

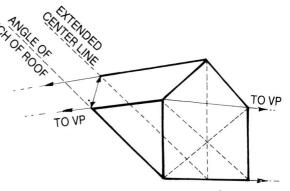

THREE-POINT PERSPECTIVE . . .

When we view an object from the top, we are most likely viewing it in three-point perspective. Most often we are able to draw this view without worrying too much about the third point, but if the object is viewed at such an angle as to make the sides appear to be oblique from side to side *and* top to bottom, then we must use the third point. A good example of three-point perspective is to look at a tall building from either a top view or a bottom view as shown below.

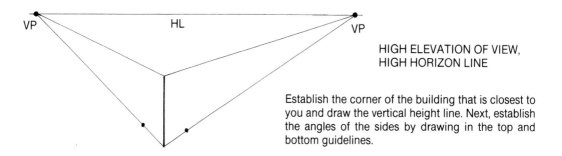

HIGH ELEVATION OF VIEW,
HIGH HORIZON LINE

Establish the corner of the building that is closest to you and draw the vertical height line. Next, establish the angles of the sides by drawing in the top and bottom guidelines.

Using visual measurements, establish the bottom width of each side by placing dots on the bottom lines.

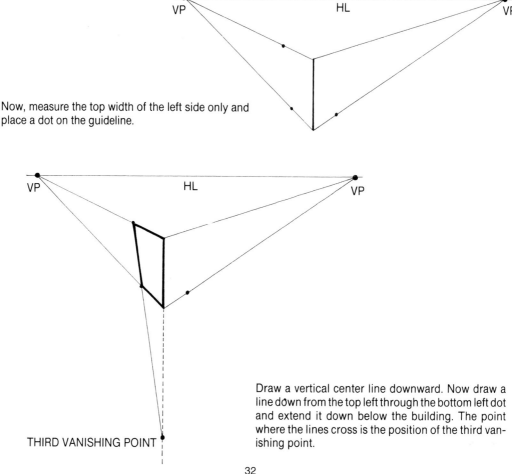

Now, measure the top width of the left side only and place a dot on the guideline.

THIRD VANISHING POINT

Draw a vertical center line downward. Now draw a line down from the top left through the bottom left dot and extend it down below the building. The point where the lines cross is the position of the third vanishing point.

32

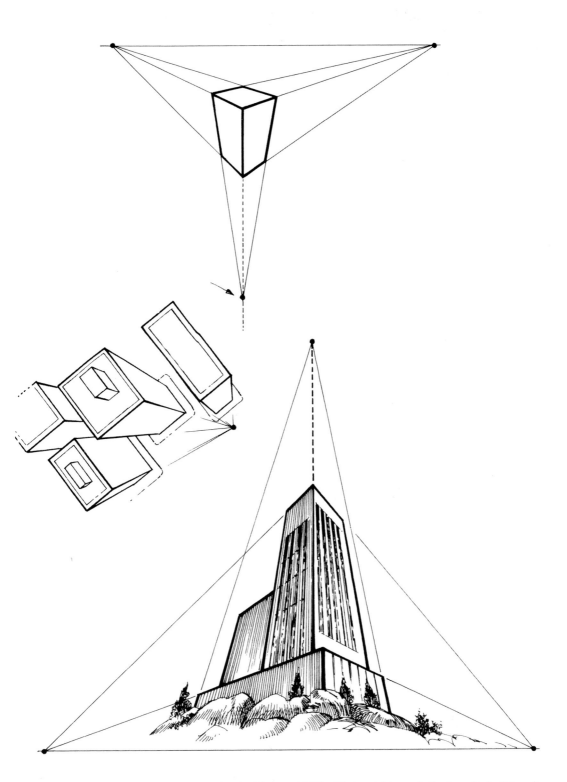

Here is an example of a building from a view looking up at it. The third vanishing point is above the building. A general rule of perspective is that all vertical lines be kept truly vertical unless three-point perspective is used for dramatic effects. Three-point perspective can be a tremendous aid in making dramatic presentations in our pictures.

DRAWING ELLIPSES . . .

An ellipse is a circle that is viewed other than straight on. When we look across the surface of the face of the circle, it is foreshortened and we see an ellipse. No matter what degree of angle the ellipse is viewed, one dimension will always remain constant with the circle. The constant (the axis) is a straight line through the circle and ellipse upon which it supposedly or actually rotates like a spinning coin.

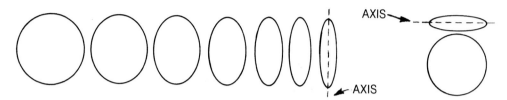

Here are a number of ellipses at various degrees of angles. Notice that the height is constant with the circle on the left.

It is important to draw ellipses correctly. If not, any object they are a part of will appear distorted. The top of a glass, a cylinder, a lampshade, a tin can, and a vase are all examples of ellipses.

Here is an exercise that shows how to build an ellipse using the circle as a guide.

The easiest way to start is to place a circle into a square. By doing this, we have edges that we can use for measurements. The circle is uniform in measurement and so is the square. Together, they become the perfect tool.

When drawing the ellipse from your subject, it is best to sketch it in freehand. Then use the following method to prove or correct it.

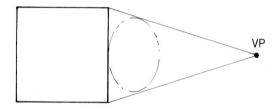

First, from the vanishing point and the top and bottom of the sketched ellipse, project lines across to the edge of a separate piece of paper. Draw two horizontal lines from the point of contact with the paper's edge. This is the height of the square. Now, draw two vertical lines the same distance apart as the height lines and we have the square established in relation to the sketched ellipse.

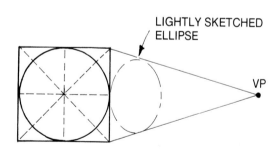

LIGHTLY SKETCHED ELLIPSE

VP

Now, divide the square in the manner shown, using the methods we have already studied. Then, fill the square with a circle.

Place points where the circle crosses the division lines. Then, extend two lines to the right from these points to the edge of the square.

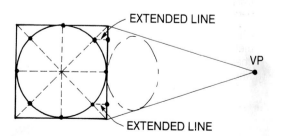

EXTENDED LINE

VP

EXTENDED LINE

Next, draw the back edge of the ellipse using eye measurement for width. Then, divide this perspective square like the flat square.

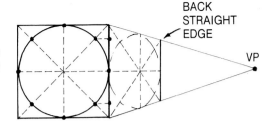

BACK
STRAIGHT
EDGE

VP

Now draw perspective lines from the three points at the edge of the square to the vanishing point. Next, place a dot at each point where the lines cross the division lines. Now we have a set of points to use in checking and drawing the ellipse in proper perspective.

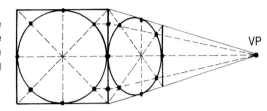

VP

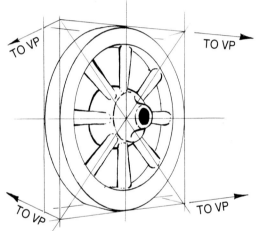

TO VP

TO VP

TO VP

TO VP

For this wagon wheel, a square in perspective was drawn as the outer boundary. Then it was divided in the same manner as before. Then, the circle/ellipse was drawn in it using a separate piece of paper as a tool. Like above, at the cross points, the ellipse was drawn.

The spokes are placed by using the division lines as guides. Simply extend the hub outward using the vanishing point and draw smaller ellipses.

The closer the ellipse is to eye level, the flatter it appears. As it moves down and away from eye level, we see more of the face of the ellipse. In order to make each one correct, we must first place it into a perspective plane then work out the different planes as shown here.

After the planes are established, by using the same methods used previously, we establish the points to check and draw a very correct ellipse into the plane where it is located.

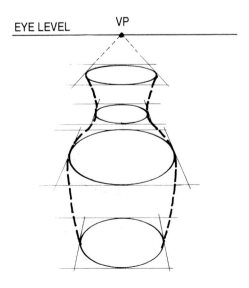

EYE LEVEL   VP

FORESHORTENING . . .

According to Webster's Dictionary, "foreshortening" means, "to represent the lines of (an object) as shorter than they actually are in order to give the illusion of proper relative size, in accordance with the principles of perspective." Here are a few simple examples of foreshortening to practice.

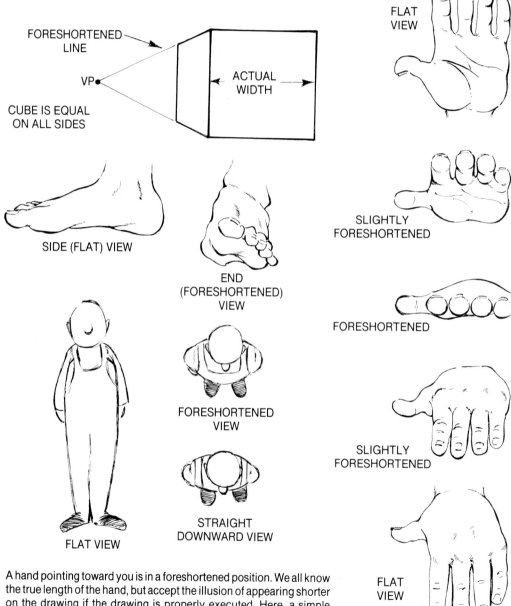

FORESHORTENED LINE

VP

ACTUAL WIDTH

CUBE IS EQUAL ON ALL SIDES

FLAT VIEW

SIDE (FLAT) VIEW

END (FORESHORTENED) VIEW

SLIGHTLY FORESHORTENED

FORESHORTENED

FORESHORTENED VIEW

STRAIGHT DOWNWARD VIEW

FLAT VIEW

SLIGHTLY FORESHORTENED

FLAT VIEW

A hand pointing toward you is in a foreshortened position. We all know the true length of the hand, but accept the illusion of appearing shorter on the drawing if the drawing is properly executed. Here, a simple cartoon hand is shown in various positions of foreshortening. Try to fit the objects into block forms as guides at first. The more you practice, the easier foreshortening will become. Pretty soon, there will be no need for the block-in guides; freehand sketching will do it all!

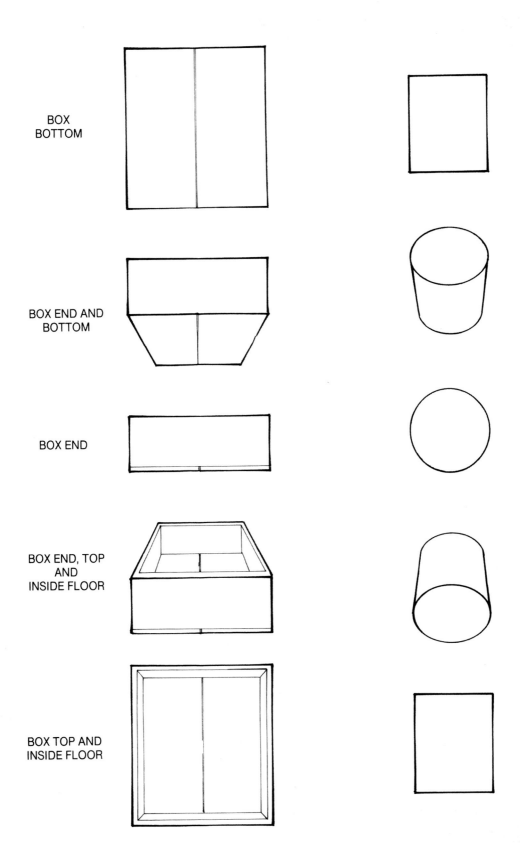

BOX
BOTTOM

BOX END AND
BOTTOM

BOX END

BOX END, TOP
AND
INSIDE FLOOR

BOX TOP AND
INSIDE FLOOR

DRAWING PEOPLE
IN PERSPECTIVE . . .

If we place figures at random in our picture and do not measure them one against the other we will probably end up with some of the figures out of proportion and some possibly appearing to float.

People are of a general height and the minute a figure is placed in the picture we automatically judge the size of all other objects by it. Figures that are placed more distant than others will appear smaller. The farther they are placed from the viewer, the smaller they will be.

It is simple to create a drawing with all of the figures in correct proportion to one another and to all other objects in the picture. Here are some exercises showing the methods.

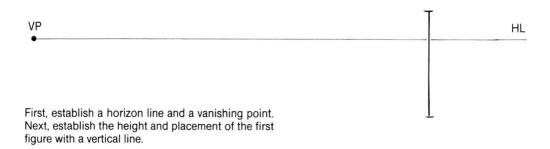

First, establish a horizon line and a vanishing point. Next, establish the height and placement of the first figure with a vertical line.

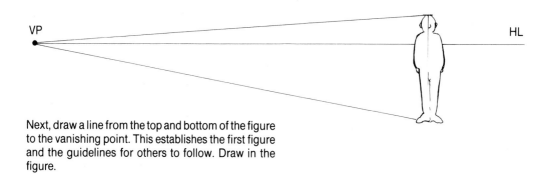

Next, draw a line from the top and bottom of the figure to the vanishing point. This establishes the first figure and the guidelines for others to follow. Draw in the figure.

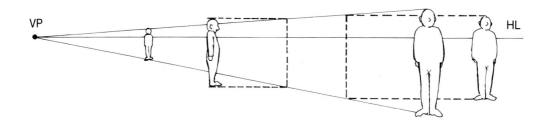

Next, using the first figure and the guidelines, draw in other figures in different places. The vertical distance between the top and bottom lines establishes the height for all of the other figures. This, of course, is for standing figures.

Here we see another example of this simple method of measuring figures and placing them in their proper heights for the position in the picture.

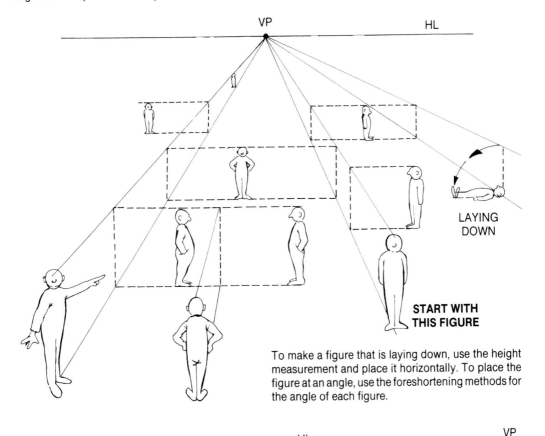

VP   HL

LAYING DOWN

START WITH THIS FIGURE

To make a figure that is laying down, use the height measurement and place it horizontally. To place the figure at an angle, use the foreshortening methods for the angle of each figure.

HL   VP

AN AVERAGE ADULT IS 7½ HEADS TALL, BUT AN ARTISTIC FIGURE IS DRAWN 8 HEADS TALL.

When we need to be exact with differing parts of the figure, simply divide the height into equal parts. A general guide for the artistic figure is 8 heads tall. Use this graph as a guide for the other figures and for drawing children. When drawing figures that are sitting or lounging, visually measure heights and postures. Use your established figures as a reference and sketch in the proper foreshortening. By using this method of measuring the correct heights of figures, we can see that our subject and the number of people can be endless.

Practice some exercises of your own — it's fun! Again, the more you practice, the less you need to use these guidelines. After awhile, it becomes second nature. Then we will only use this to check and correct any errors in our work.

8 HEADS TALL

5 YEAR OLD

A 5-YEAR OLD EQUALS ABOUT 4½ ADULT HEADS IN HEIGHT.

Changing Elevations

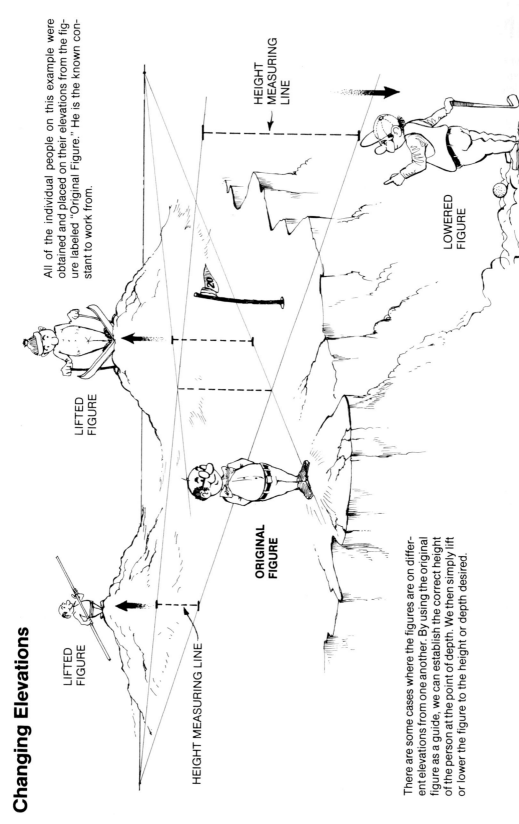

All of the individual people on this example were obtained and placed on their elevations from the figure labeled "Original Figure." He is the known constant to work from.

HEIGHT MEASURING LINE

LOWERED FIGURE

LIFTED FIGURE

ORIGINAL FIGURE

LIFTED FIGURE

HEIGHT MEASURING LINE

There are some cases where the figures are on different elevations from one another. By using the original figure as a guide, we can establish the correct height of the person at the point of depth. We then simply lift or lower the figure to the height or depth desired.

CASTING SHADOWS
IN PERSPECTIVE . . .

When we have a single light source, all of the shadows in the picture recede to the same vanishing point. This vanishing point is placed directly under the light source, whether on the horizon line or more forward in the picture. The shadows follow the plane on which the object is sitting. Shadows also follow the contour of the plane on which they are cast.

Light rays travel in straight lines and strike an object that is in the way. That object then blocks the rays from continuing onward. This creates the absence of light in the form of a shadow. Each shadow has its own shape that is peculiar to the object that casts it. Notice the different shapes of shadows in all of the following examples.

● LIGHT
SOURCE

Step 1. Draw a cube using two-point perspective. Next, select a point for the light source and place a dot there.

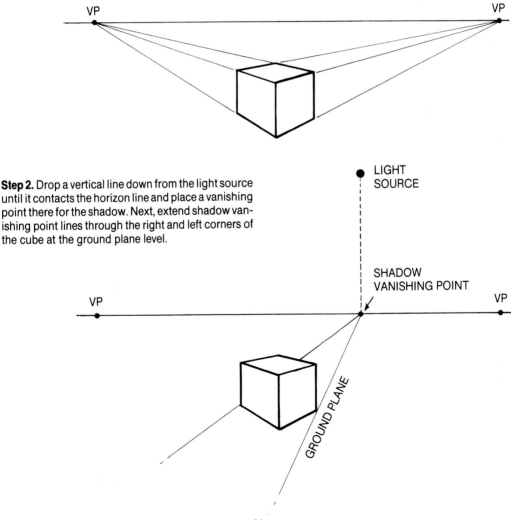

Step 2. Drop a vertical line down from the light source until it contacts the horizon line and place a vanishing point there for the shadow. Next, extend shadow vanishing point lines through the right and left corners of the cube at the ground plane level.

LIGHT
SOURCE

SHADOW
VANISHING POINT

VP

VP

GROUND PLANE

Step 3. Next, draw light direction lines A, B and C from the light source and touch the three forward corners of the cube, extending onward. The length of the shadow is set where the shadow vanishing point lines and the light direction lines cross. Now, draw a projection line for the side to the right object vanishing point.

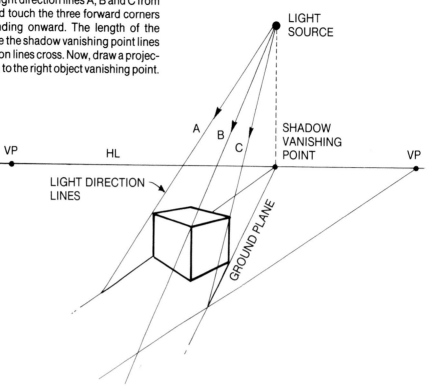

Step 4. Now draw a line from the left object vanishing point through the point where the light line A and the left shadow vanishing point line cross. This gives the depth of the shadow. Shade in the shadow. Notice the odd shape of the shadow cast by the cube.

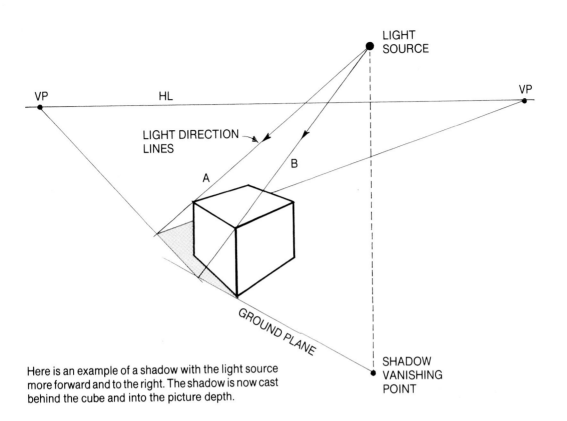

Here is an example of a shadow with the light source more forward and to the right. The shadow is now cast behind the cube and into the picture depth.

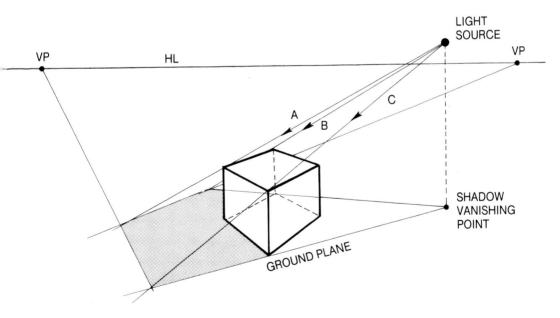

Here the light is changed again. Notice the strange shape of the shadow. It is important to pay close attention to the shape of shadows in order to make our drawing and painting realistic and true.

Finding the Length of a Cast Shadow

The higher the light source, the shorter the shadow. The more directly overhead the light source is, the shorter the shadow. Here are a few examples of lengths of shadows depending upon the position of the light source. At morning and late afternoon, the shadows are longer and more dramatic due to the low angle of light. At noon, they are shorter because the light is in a higher position.

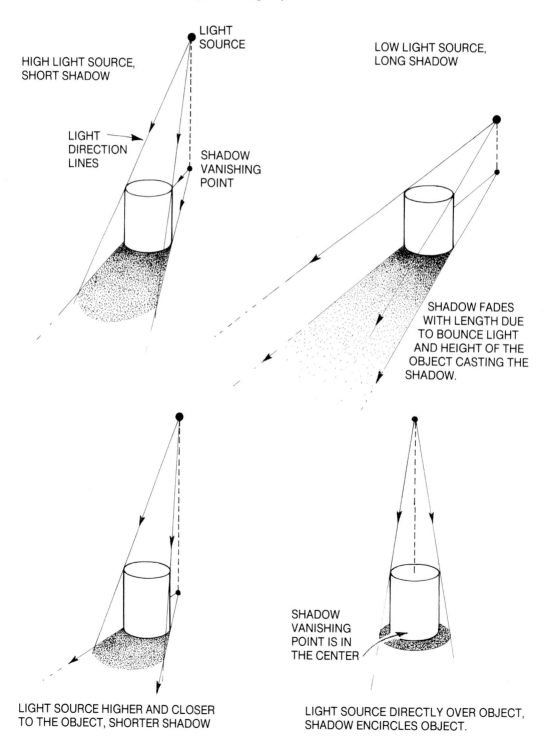

LIGHT SOURCE

HIGH LIGHT SOURCE, SHORT SHADOW

LOW LIGHT SOURCE, LONG SHADOW

LIGHT DIRECTION LINES

SHADOW VANISHING POINT

SHADOW FADES WITH LENGTH DUE TO BOUNCE LIGHT AND HEIGHT OF THE OBJECT CASTING THE SHADOW.

SHADOW VANISHING POINT IS IN THE CENTER

LIGHT SOURCE HIGHER AND CLOSER TO THE OBJECT, SHORTER SHADOW

LIGHT SOURCE DIRECTLY OVER OBJECT, SHADOW ENCIRCLES OBJECT.

If the light source point happens to fall behind and directly in line with the object, like the fence post in the example, we can find the correct length of the shadow by moving the height of the fence post to one side. Then, using the method shown here, we find the length of the shadow and move it back into place.

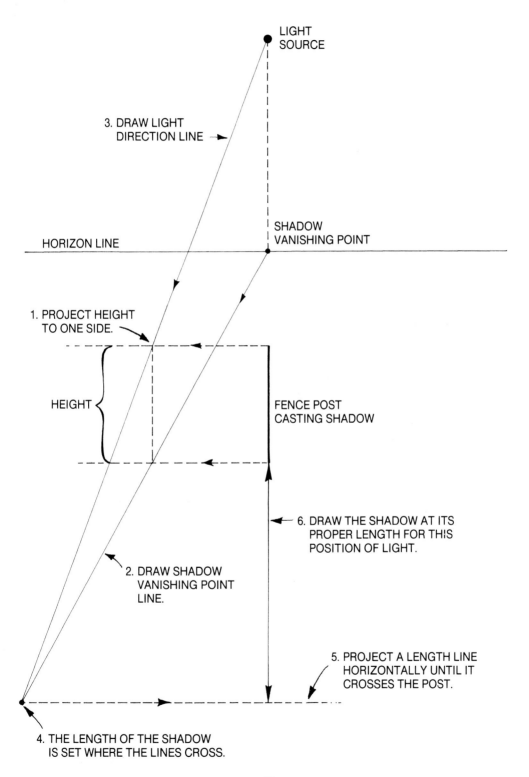

LIGHT
SOURCE

3. DRAW LIGHT
DIRECTION LINE →

SHADOW
VANISHING POINT

HORIZON LINE

1. PROJECT HEIGHT
TO ONE SIDE.

HEIGHT

FENCE POST
CASTING SHADOW

6. DRAW THE SHADOW AT ITS
PROPER LENGTH FOR THIS
POSITION OF LIGHT.

2. DRAW SHADOW
VANISHING POINT
LINE.

5. PROJECT A LENGTH LINE
HORIZONTALLY UNTIL IT
CROSSES THE POST.

4. THE LENGTH OF THE SHADOW
IS SET WHERE THE LINES CROSS.

REFLECTIONS
IN PERSPECTIVE . . .

If we place a mirror under an object, the mirror will reflect the object in the way very calm water will. There are several things to consider, however, when studying reflections. The closer an object is to us in the picture plane, the more we look down at it, and the more a mirror looks up at it. A reflection is *not* just an upside down version of the object, it is another view altogether. The closer the object is to eye level and the horizon line, the closer the duplication of it will be. However, the circumstances of viewing would have to be perfectly equal in order to create a duplicate view, or an upside down object. This very rarely occurs.

Also, a reflected object will reflect in a mirror or calm water only as deep as it is tall. The only time this will change is if the surface of the water is moving or rippled, breaking up the reflection and extending it. Study the following examples very closely.

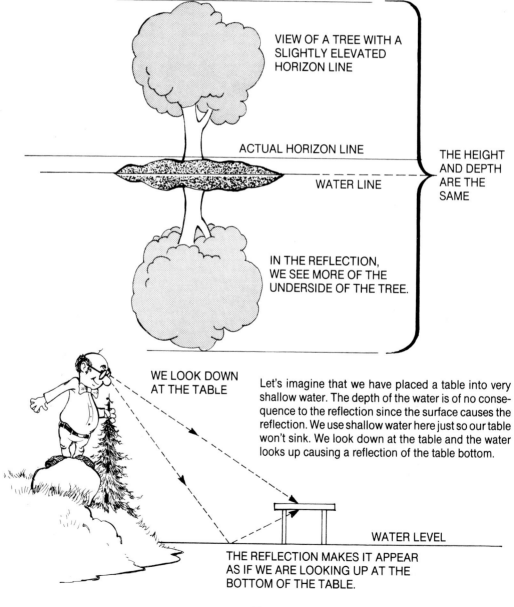

VIEW OF A TREE WITH A
SLIGHTLY ELEVATED
HORIZON LINE

ACTUAL HORIZON LINE

WATER LINE

THE HEIGHT
AND DEPTH
ARE THE
SAME

IN THE REFLECTION,
WE SEE MORE OF THE
UNDERSIDE OF THE TREE.

WE LOOK DOWN
AT THE TABLE

Let's imagine that we have placed a table into very shallow water. The depth of the water is of no consequence to the reflection since the surface causes the reflection. We use shallow water here just so our table won't sink. We look down at the table and the water looks up causing a reflection of the table bottom.

WATER LEVEL

THE REFLECTION MAKES IT APPEAR
AS IF WE ARE LOOKING UP AT THE
BOTTOM OF THE TABLE.

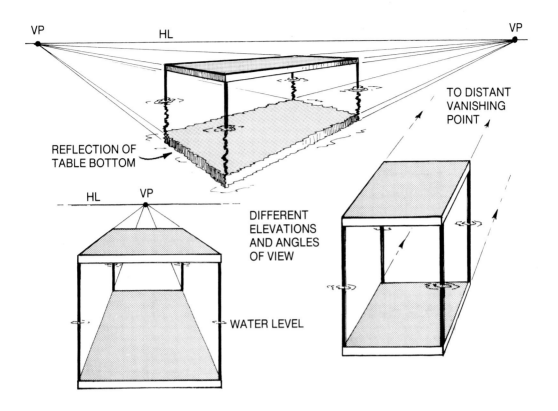

VP

HL

VP

TO DISTANT
VANISHING
POINT

REFLECTION OF
TABLE BOTTOM

HL   VP

DIFFERENT
ELEVATIONS
AND ANGLES
OF VIEW

WATER LEVEL

Here are some examples of reflections of objects proving that reflections cannot be just reversed drawings.

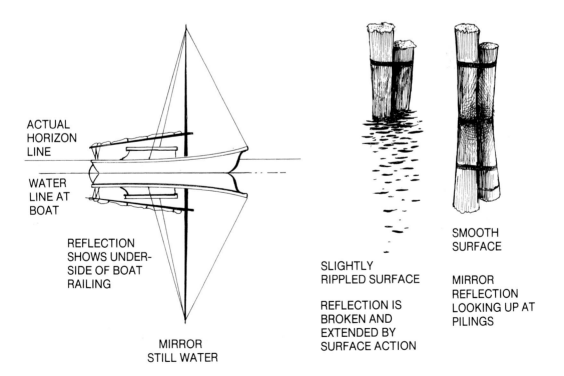

ACTUAL
HORIZON
LINE

WATER
LINE AT
BOAT

REFLECTION
SHOWS UNDER-
SIDE OF BOAT
RAILING

MIRROR
STILL WATER

SLIGHTLY
RIPPLED SURFACE

REFLECTION IS
BROKEN AND
EXTENDED BY
SURFACE ACTION

SMOOTH
SURFACE

MIRROR
REFLECTION
LOOKING UP AT
PILINGS

CHANGING PLANES AND DIRECTIONS . . .

A wandering road not only changes direction, but, as it winds back and forth, it also changes elevations depending on the ground plane. In order to represent this correctly in our drawing, we use the following methods as guides. After establishing the directions of the roads, simply round the points at the curves for a natural look.

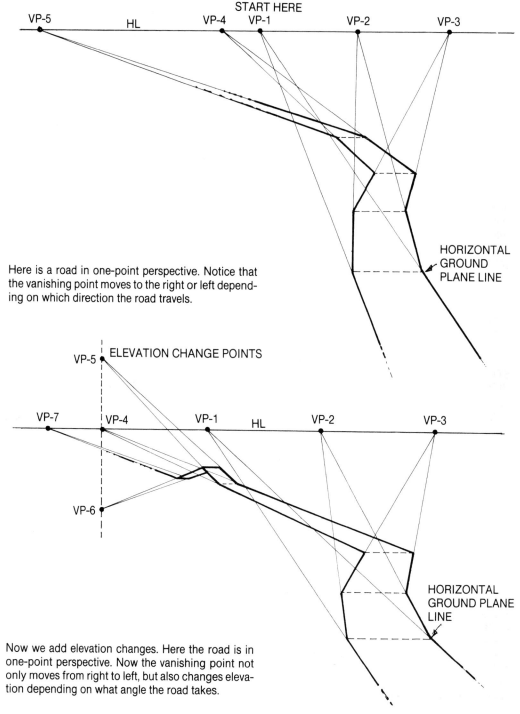

START HERE

VP-5　　　　HL　　　　VP-4　VP-1　　　　VP-2　　　　VP-3

HORIZONTAL GROUND PLANE LINE

Here is a road in one-point perspective. Notice that the vanishing point moves to the right or left depending on which direction the road travels.

ELEVATION CHANGE POINTS

VP-5

VP-7　　　VP-4　　　　VP-1　　HL　　　VP-2　　　　VP-3

VP-6

HORIZONTAL GROUND PLANE LINE

Now we add elevation changes. Here the road is in one-point perspective. Now the vanishing point not only moves from right to left, but also changes elevation depending on what angle the road takes.

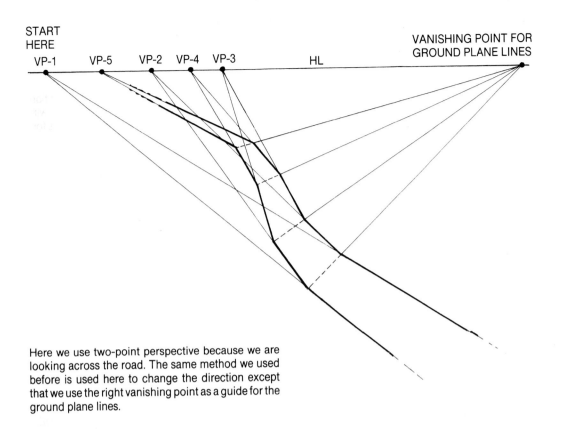

START
HERE
VP-1   VP-5   VP-2   VP-4   VP-3   HL

VANISHING POINT FOR
GROUND PLANE LINES

Here we use two-point perspective because we are looking across the road. The same method we used before is used here to change the direction except that we use the right vanishing point as a guide for the ground plane lines.

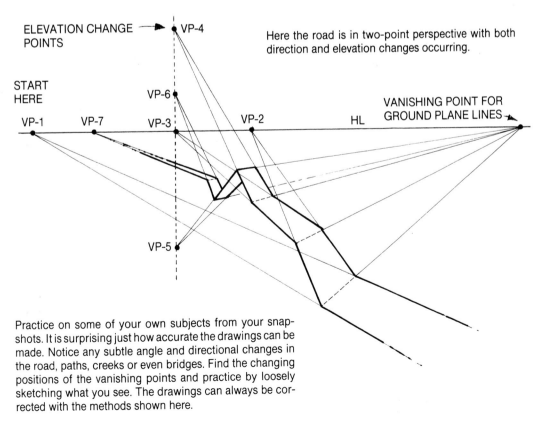

ELEVATION CHANGE ➔ VP-4
POINTS

Here the road is in two-point perspective with both direction and elevation changes occurring.

START
HERE

VP-6

VP-1   VP-7   VP-3   VP-2   HL

VANISHING POINT FOR
GROUND PLANE LINES ➔

VP-5

Practice on some of your own subjects from your snapshots. It is surprising just how accurate the drawings can be made. Notice any subtle angle and directional changes in the road, paths, creeks or even bridges. Find the changing positions of the vanishing points and practice by loosely sketching what you see. The drawings can always be corrected with the methods shown here.

PERSPECTIVE FROM A PLAN DRAWING . . .

There are times when you might like to visualize what an object might look like when the only material you have is a plan of it. By using the following method, a dimensional perspective view can be drawn. It is easy if taken step-by-step. Let's draw a house together.

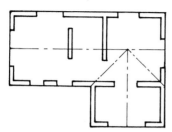

Here we have the simplified downward plan view of a small house. This shows the length and width of the house.

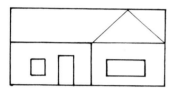

Here is what is known as an elevation view of the same house. It shows the height of the roof, windows, doors and outside walls.

In order to obtain a dimensional view of the house, we must use both of the above views. Follow the steps in the order given and we can do just that with ease.

Step 1. Draw a horizontal line and label it "Picture Plane."

Step 2. Place the plan on the line so that the areas you want to see in the drawing are facing the picture plane line and the corner closest to you touches the line.

PLAN VIEW

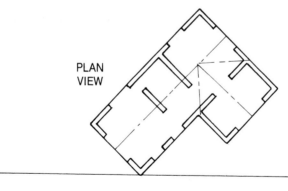

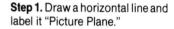

PICTURE PLANE

Step 3. Place the elevation view to the right of where the perspective drawing will be and draw a horizontal "Ground Line."

ELEVATION VIEW

HORIZONTAL GROUND LINE

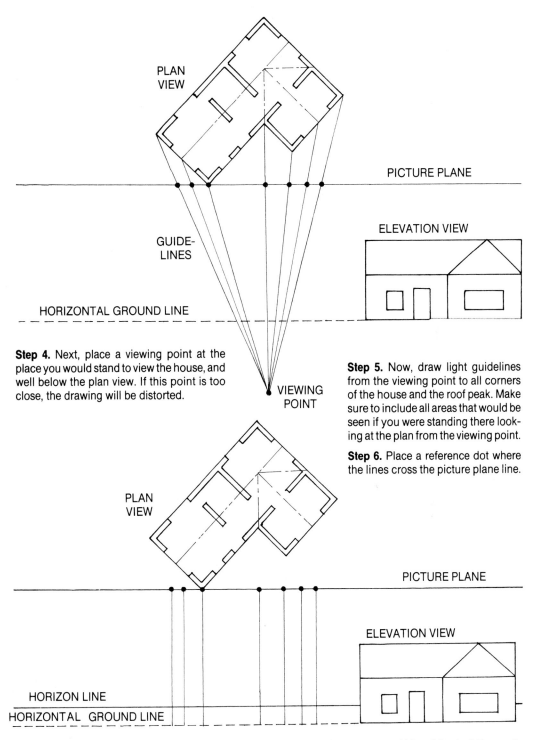

PLAN VIEW

PICTURE PLANE

ELEVATION VIEW

GUIDE-LINES

HORIZONTAL GROUND LINE

Step 4. Next, place a viewing point at the place you would stand to view the house, and well below the plan view. If this point is too close, the drawing will be distorted.

VIEWING POINT

Step 5. Now, draw light guidelines from the viewing point to all corners of the house and the roof peak. Make sure to include all areas that would be seen if you were standing there looking at the plan from the viewing point.

Step 6. Place a reference dot where the lines cross the picture plane line.

PLAN VIEW

PICTURE PLANE

ELEVATION VIEW

HORIZON LINE

HORIZONTAL GROUND LINE

Step 7. From these dots, draw parallel vertical lines which locate the accurate widths of the building walls right down to the horizontal ground line.

Step 8. Now establish the horizon line for the elevation of view you wish to portray. It can vary. I have placed this one at a normal viewing position, about halfway through the height of the elevation view. At this point, I have eliminated the guidelines since they have already served their purpose and to make the illustration less confusing.

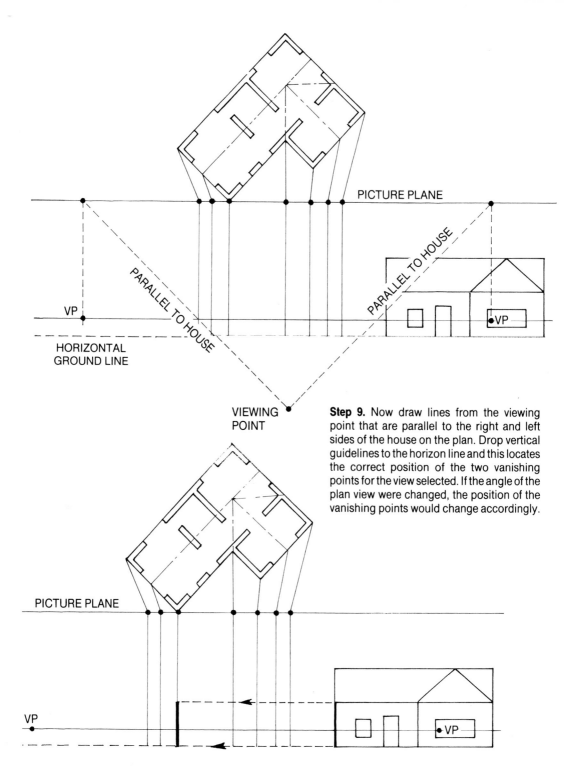

PICTURE PLANE

PARALLEL TO HOUSE

PARALLEL TO HOUSE

VP

HORIZONTAL
GROUND LINE

VP

VIEWING
POINT

Step 9. Now draw lines from the viewing point that are parallel to the right and left sides of the house on the plan. Drop vertical guidelines to the horizon line and this locates the correct position of the two vanishing points for the view selected. If the angle of the plan view were changed, the position of the vanishing points would change accordingly.

PICTURE PLANE

VP

VP

Step 10. The only line that we can use for measurement from the elevation view is the one at the corner that is nearest to us. I have marked this line thicker than the rest so that you can easily see it compared with the rest of the drawing. With this in mind, lightly extend the height reference lines from the top and bottom of this corner line, across the drawing area. ANY AND ALL HEIGHT MEASUREMENTS CAN BE MADE FROM THE ELEVATION VIEW, WINDOWS, DOORS, ETC., by extending them in the same manner to this corner line, then using the vanishing points, working them into their proper positions.

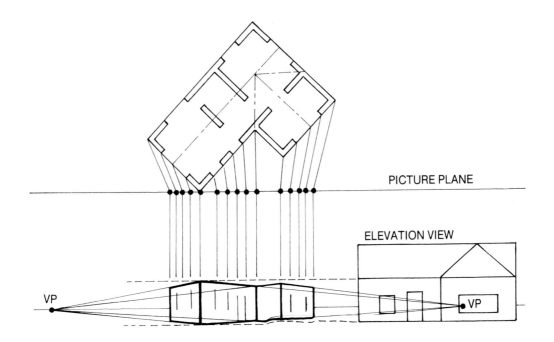

Step 11. Now draw in the perspective view of the walls using the two vanishing points and the rules already studied. Using two-point perspective, start with the front corner line and develop the house from there. Draw in the vertical lines as guides for the widths of the windows and the door.

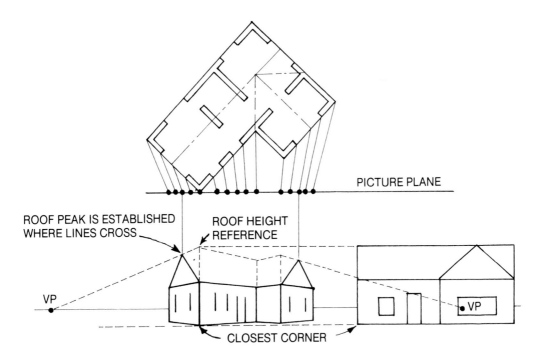

Step 12. The angle for the peak of the roof is obtained by extending the roof height line over to the same vertical corner measuring line. Use the vanishing points to find the height of the LEFT peak first. Then, using the vanishing points, draw a phantom height extension over to the right peak, following the angles of the walls. Establish the height of the peak from the point where the vertical line and the phantom line cross.

Step 13. After establishing the two peaks, draw in the rest of the roof. Since the window and door width guidelines are already in place, we no longer need the plan view.

Step 14. All that is needed now are the height measurements for the windows and door. Extend these guidelines from the elevation view to the front corner line, as shown.

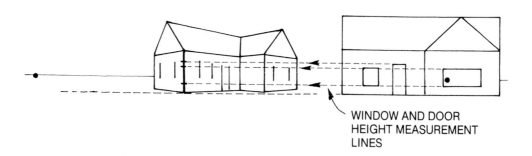

WINDOW AND DOOR
HEIGHT MEASUREMENT
LINES

From the height measurement guidelines, use the vanishing points and project the heights around the house to the proper place. Then, firmly draw in the door and the windows.

We now have the basic form for a simple house to build on. It can be drawn as complexly or as simply as desired. Whatever technique of shading and texturing we choose, we have a foundation that is correct in proportions and, most of all, perspective. Have fun! It is a rare occasion that this type of perspective drawing would be used in freehand sketching, but it is very important to understand the principles of it. This is the type of procedure followed by persons in drafting and architecture. Even so, a good all-around artist should have this knowledge to use when needed.

Exercise to Practice

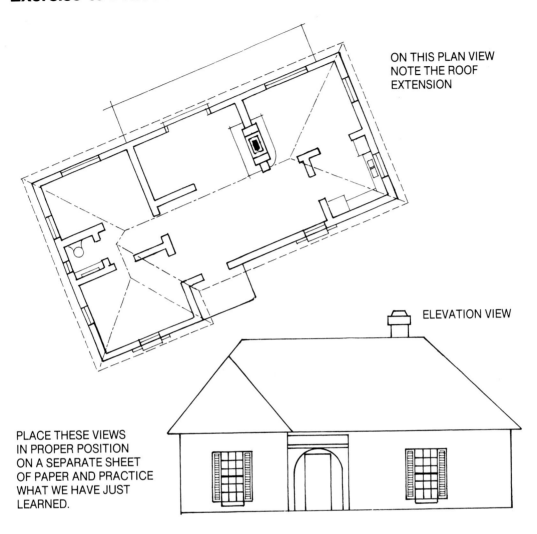

ON THIS PLAN VIEW
NOTE THE ROOF
EXTENSION

ELEVATION VIEW

PLACE THESE VIEWS
IN PROPER POSITION
ON A SEPARATE SHEET
OF PAPER AND PRACTICE
WHAT WE HAVE JUST
LEARNED.

THINGS TO REMEMBER: PICTURE PLANE, HORIZONTAL GROUND LINE, VIEWING
POINT, HORIZON LINE, GUIDELINES, VERTICAL LINES, EXTENDED HEIGHT
REFERENCE LINES, ROOF PEAK.

COMPLEX AND IRREGULAR FORMS IN PERSPECTIVE . . .

As we know, there are four basic forms — the cube, the cylinder, the cone and the sphere. Almost every object can be related to a cubic form, including the human head and body. Some shapes are a composition of many cubes. Some, however, do not relate to the cube. In this instance, we use either the cone, the cylinder or the sphere. Upon observation, we find that some objects are also a combination of several of these basic forms.

Exercises to Practice

My old West Virginia whiskey jug is a combination of cylinder and cone, with an ellipse on the top, the middle and the bottom. The handle is one of those irregular forms that is best drawn by eye. In order to draw the handle in perspective, we would employ the same method used in the changing angles and elevations of the road.

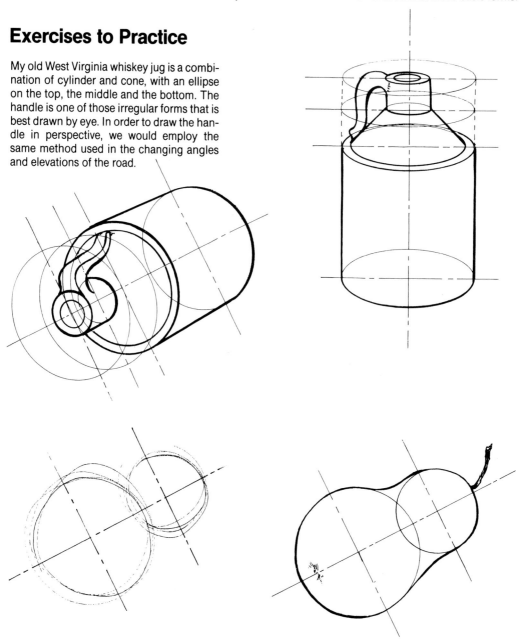

Using these forms as basic guides for sketching is a great aid. After we have the general shape of the object sketched in, we can check it for accuracy, if necessary, by using the rules of perspective we have learned.

In views that depart from the "norm" and are considered unusual, or views that are changing, it is very helpful to place the object into a rectangle that houses it comfortably. This will give us a general guide to be used in checking for accuracy. When checking, always refer to the three most important parts of perspective: viewing level and angle, eye level or horizon line, and vanishing point or points.

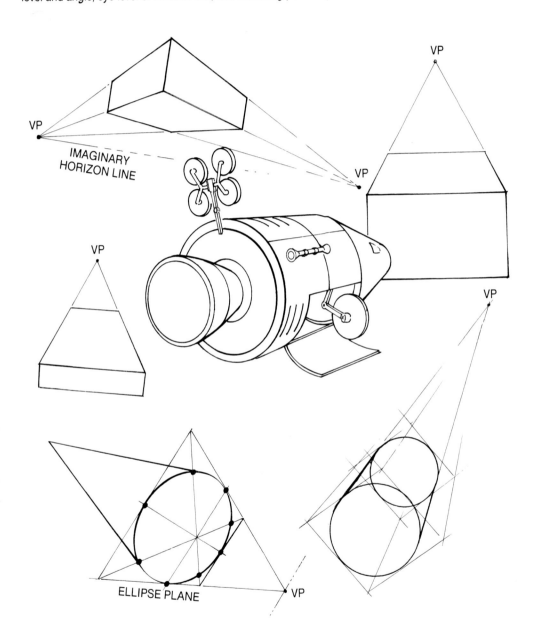

Here are several forms floating in space. Notice that each has its own imaginary horizon line and set of vanishing points. This is the type of perspective theory used in illustrations of objects floating in outer space. The horizon line is imaginary, but necessary for keeping proportions of objects correct.

Here is a good example of how a complex object like the human head can be compared to a block form for perspective purposes.

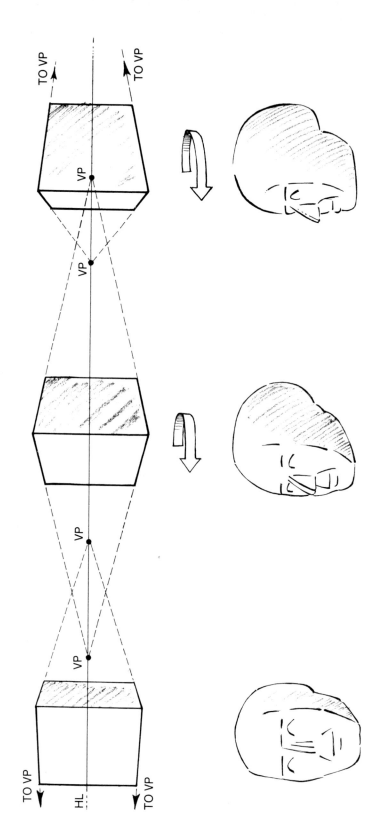

ENHANCING DEPTH BY SHADING AND TEXTURING . . .

Here we have rocks and distant trees drawn in ink line only. They have the suggestion of depth due to the direction of lines. Irregular and uneven forms like these are difficult to show very much perspective depth when just in line form.

Here we have the same rocks and trees, but they have been shaded and textured with a pencil. I used a pencil with a lead of "HB" hardness. Notice that the tree on the left appears more distant than the large one due to shading it in a lighter tone.

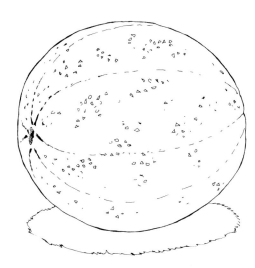

Here, again, the line direction gives us a feeling of direction and form. It is limited unless we texture and shade it further in ink. In ink shading, we do not have the soft graduations of tone value as with pencil.

Now we see the depth of the melon along with the textured surface. Remember that each object catches light and casts shadows according to its form. It also has a surface texture that is unique to itself. A felt hat and a straw hat are both hats, but each has a different surface texture.

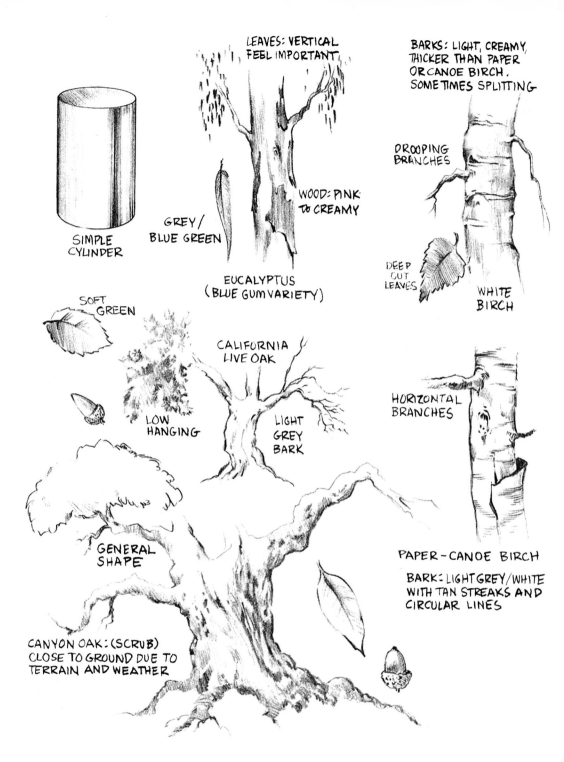

LEAVES: VERTICAL
FEEL IMPORTANT

BARKS: LIGHT, CREAMY,
THICKER THAN PAPER
OR CANOE BIRCH.
SOMETIMES SPLITTING

DROOPING
BRANCHES

WOOD: PINK·
TO CREAMY

GREY /
BLUE GREEN

DEEP
CUT
LEAVES

WHITE
BIRCH

SIMPLE
CYLINDER

EUCALYPTUS
(BLUE GUM VARIETY)

SOFT
GREEN

CALIFORNIA
LIVE OAK

HORIZONTAL
BRANCHES

LOW
HANGING

LIGHT
GREY
BARK

GENERAL
SHAPE

PAPER – CANOE BIRCH

BARK: LIGHT GREY/WHITE
WITH TAN STREAKS AND
CIRCULAR LINES

CANYON OAK: (SCRUB)
CLOSE TO GROUND DUE TO
TERRAIN AND WEATHER

In this set of sketches of various trees sketched while on a field trip, I have added the drawing of a cylinder to compare with the round shape of the tree trunks. The light and dark graduations of tone are drawn vertically. These give the illusion of depth and roundness. The same basic shading techniques are used for the tree trunks. Any unevenness or roughness in the bark of the trees is indicated by the change in direction of line and shading. However, the *overall* shading of the cylindrical trunk is still vertical.

Light, Atmosphere and Moisture

The sky sets the mood of the painting because it controls the light and color used. Clouds filter light when they are dense, and soften value changes. They accent sky colors when broken and bright.

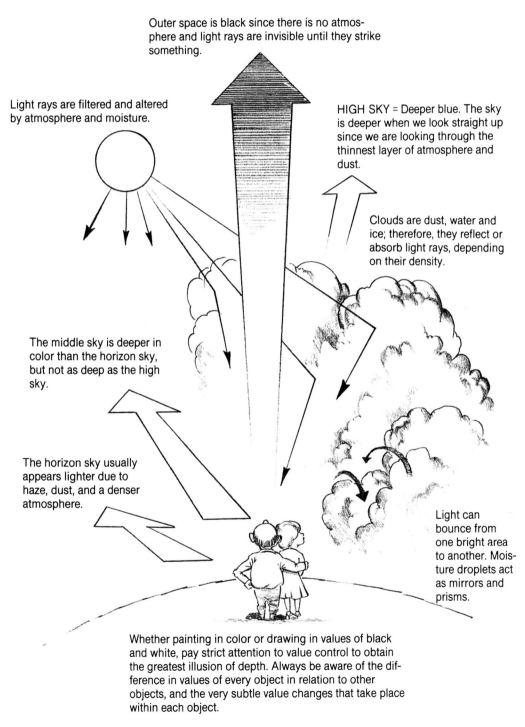

Outer space is black since there is no atmosphere and light rays are invisible until they strike something.

Light rays are filtered and altered by atmosphere and moisture.

HIGH SKY = Deeper blue. The sky is deeper when we look straight up since we are looking through the thinnest layer of atmosphere and dust.

Clouds are dust, water and ice; therefore, they reflect or absorb light rays, depending on their density.

The middle sky is deeper in color than the horizon sky, but not as deep as the high sky.

The horizon sky usually appears lighter due to haze, dust, and a denser atmosphere.

Light can bounce from one bright area to another. Moisture droplets act as mirrors and prisms.

Whether painting in color or drawing in values of black and white, pay strict attention to value control to obtain the greatest illusion of depth. Always be aware of the difference in values of every object in relation to other objects, and the very subtle value changes that take place within each object.

Not only do we create the illusion of depth through value changes with texturing and shading, but another good method is the placement of objects within the composition so as to overlap one another. The object that is overlapped will always appear to be more distant, so we obtain depth in our picture. These three pencil sketches are roughs done as preliminaries for paintings. Notice that even in rough sketches, the direction of stroke for texture and lightness or darkness is important to the illusion of perspective depth.

Usually, distant objects appear lighter in value than close objects. Sometimes, however, in a very complex composition using color, a dark color can either come forward or recede. It depends on how we use it. Be thoughtful with color values too. See *The World of Color And How To Use It*," Book #5 in Walter Foster's Artist's Library Series.

Exercises to Practice

The photo at the left is the archway at Mission San Luis Rey, in California. Notice that the arches, wooden beams, and the bricks on the flooring all move into the picture to one vanishing point. Also note the depth that is obtained in nature by the overlapping of forms. The open archway at the end appears to be very small and so do the people under it. Use this photo as an exercise and find the horizon line and vanishing point. Then, draw the arches using the method for ellipses to get the proper graceful curves of the arches on the right. Take your time. We have studied everything that you will need to draw this scene.

The photo on the right shows the beauty and grace of part of the Organ Pavillion in Balboa Park, San Diego, California. To draw this angle of view, we could use the same methods used on page 48 for changing directions of roads. Great depth is shown by the dramatic overlapping of the vertical columns.

Study these two paintings and the four on the next page and notice that even though the original paintings are in color, we can still see depth in these black and white photos by the changes in values of darks and light and the overlapping of forms. Dark and light create form. Shapes and value changes give the illusion of depth. Even though there is not great distance in the painting of the gull, rocks and foam, we see water movement and wave action by using texturing and value changes.

The above paintings are fine examples of depth with value changes. The lighthouse at Point Loma, California is a good example of a white building in various soft values of grey. This gives form and depth. Notice the overlapping of forms and subtle value changes in the others.

I hope that you have enjoyed this study in perspective and that it will always be a reference for you in your work. Remember, keep the rules of perspective simple and they will work much better.

Thank you for your interest in my work, and I wish you all of the very best in your world of drawing, painting and perspective.

William H. Powell